M000117263

"*Joyous Leadership* is a must-read for any aspiring leader. The book emphasizes the benefits, both personally and professionally, of leading with purpose. It highlights the reality that strong business performance requires team members who act and think like owners and are immersed in their daily work. Mark's experiences and simple storytelling make this an indulging read." **–Lee C. Banks, Vice Chairman & President, Parker Hannifin Corporation**

"In the process of sharing his story, he's helping me to see the joy in my own life now and for eternity. Now that's a precious gift!" **–Dr. Robert Fisher, President, Belmont University**

"*Joyous Leadership* is a great read because of Mark's storytelling abilities. Mark outlines how we can use our own life circumstances to create a joyous journey. Mark's joy is infectious and inspirational." **–Gordon Bufton, Founder Genius Creators and Bestselling Author of *The Connection Effect***

"I have had the honor to work with Mark for over 20 years and refer to him as the Dalai Lama of manufacturing. His ability to motivate others through sharing his joy for life and past learnings is as powerful as a magic wand, providing inspiration to learn and reimagine. Thank you for writing *Joyous Leadership* and passing on your experiences and legacy." **–Fred Shamburg, Founder and President of Leanovations, LLC**

"What a wonderful book! Mark's life story is truly inspirational, and his storytelling is genuine, relatable, and funny. *Joyous Leadership* is one of those rare books where the stories leave you feeling that you learned timeless lessons for living a good life without being prescriptive. Mark–thank you for sharing your story!" **–Amar Shah, Managing Partner, The Keystone Group**

"Mark shapes his own life and business experiences into a roadmap that can lead you from a pursuit of happiness to your own 'special' journey." **–Kurt Powell, Executive V.P., Customer Support and Product Strategy, BUNN Corporation**

"For more than 20 years Mark has been my friend, coach, and boss. The joy of walking together and sharing a part in these stories has been a gift of life, sense of purpose, and I've become a better leader." **–Luis Buchanan, Plant Manager, Molded Fiber Glass Mexico**

Joyous
Leadership

Joyous Leadership

Stories of Learnings Along the Way

John Mark Watson

NASHVILLE, TENNESSEE

j.brand@wbrandpub.com
ONBrand Books
www.wbrandpub.com

Cover design: designchik.net

Joyous Leadership / John Mark Watson – 1st edition

Available in Hardcover, Paperback, eBook and Kindle formats.

Hardcover ISBN: 978-1-956906-03-5
Paperback ISBN: 978-1-956906-04-2
eBook ISBN: 978-1-956906-05-9

Library of Congress Control Number: 2021922180

Table of Contents

This book is dedicated to my wife Stacie and sons Jared and Tate.
Thanks for the joyous journey!

By Dr. Robert Fisher, President, Belmont University

I first met Mark Watson about twenty-five years ago when he invited me to be involved in developing a team-oriented strategy for a manufacturing plant he was leading in Trumann, Arkansas. What I remember most clearly about that experience is that Mark was a very bright, energetic, hard-working young leader who demanded the best of himself and sought to bring the best out of others all around him. We worked together to plan a strategy to create and implement a culture of teamwork among the supervisors and the people doing the work. This effort was based on *Real Dream Teams: Seven Practices Used By World Class Teams to Achieve Extraordinary Results*, a book that I had co-authored with Bo Thomas.

What made this specific consulting gig memorable is that I walked away from the experience knowing that I had not wasted my time. So often leaders and managers delve into improvements and change as something interesting to consider, the consultant goes away, but nothing really changes. Not so with this experience. Mark took this work seriously and used these efforts to make things better for both the company and for the people who gave their best efforts to the mission. I realized then that this guy was on his way to a promising career.

Joyous Leadership follows the journey of that "promising career" as Mark Watson shares the lessons that he has learned along the way. Story after story combine to create a solid framework for a successful leadership style. One of the most powerful stories is how he came to understand that you don't have to have superstars on your team to win. His experience at that Trumann plant demonstrates that ordinary people can achieve extraordinary results—if they are committed and work together as a team. Mark writes in this book that, "There truly was joy in building a team." That is a powerful and deeply important realization.

And best of all, this whole book is about joy! Man, do we need to discover what it means to be joyful. Several years ago, my wife Judy and I co-authored a book with the title *Life is a Gift: Inspiration from the Soon Departed*. This book was based on interviews with 104 patients at Alive Hospice in Nashville, Tennessee. We asked these people, who were figuratively "sitting on the front-porch of eternity," a series of questions about their life thinking that we might be able to learn about what really matters in living from people who are very close to death. The most important take-away for me was their admonition, over and over again, that we should look for joy in our lives. We shouldn't sit around waiting for it. We shouldn't expect that we can buy it with money. We should go out and actively pursue it every moment of every day. They said that joy is all around—you just have to recognize and accept it.

Mark's gift to me and to his other readers is that he is sharing the joy that he sees all around him, especially in his life's work. And, as you can read in the Conclusion, he's doing it at a time in his life when one might be excused for not seeing the joy that can be found in the most unlikely places. In the process of sharing his story, he's helping me to see the joy in my own life now and for eternity. Now that's a precious gift!

Chasing Happiness and Finding Joy

A re you in pursuit of happiness right now? Has it been a tough year, decade, life? Maybe you began this life in the back of the line with little money, a not-so-great family, disadvantaged in some way, or somehow different from your peers. Maybe you were born with plenty of opportunity but feel you failed to capitalize on it and now feel lost and wonder what to do. Maybe you are unsure of what things are contributing to your unhappiness, you only know something is amiss.

If you do feel that way or maybe feel things could be a little better, congratulations. You are in good company. As I've journeyed through this life, I too have been this person, feeling frustrated with my efforts. I've thought, *oh well, it must be just the way things are. It's the Watson curse.* But when I looked around, I saw many of my friends and colleagues were in the same boat and seemed equally disillusioned.

I spent the early part of my career pursuing happiness only to find that it was never a fully sustainable state. Periods of success were hard to enjoy. I feared it wouldn't last or I witnessed dissatisfaction in others around me. It was draining carrying around my nugget of happiness while watching others trudging through the day, anxiously awaiting retirement, or hoping for a lottery win.

I remember thinking, "I'll be happy when . . ." But the when always changed. I don't mean to say that I was never happy because I was. I did reach periods of time in my life that I was indeed happy. But because of my definition or the conditions that I put on happiness, it took very little to take that happiness away, leaving me to begin my pursuit of it again.

Then one day I realized that my happiness was not a condition or current state, it was contained in the pursuit. It was the process of overcoming struggles, adversity, and maybe even a set-back or two that was my greatest satisfaction. Prior to this understanding, I had settled for temporary happiness because much of that had been modeled in the world around me. Through some maturity, self-evaluation, and good mentors, I finally reframed my pursuit to joy. That's when things started to make sense. That's when my compass was finally pointing toward true north.

You see, there is a difference between happiness and joy, but we usually pursue both as if they are the same. Happiness is good, even necessary, but not sustainable twenty-four hours a day. Happiness is the dopamine hit we crave and get when good things happen. Joy is what sustains us between those hits. Joy is a choice and purposefully made. Happiness is more external, while joy is internal and much deeper. Joy is a skill, an art—it must be studied and learned.

One of the most beautiful phenomena is when light is refracted to make a rainbow. We can view this in nature after rain or through a manmade glass prism. By passing from air into the atmosphere or glass of the prism, the speed of light changes causing it to be refracted or bent, entering a new medium at a different angle. The degree of bending creates different wavelengths and changes ordinary white light into a spectrum of colors. It's the bending and the angles that create the beauty. Similarly, it's not our starting point in life that creates joy. We are all exposed to the same white and colorless light. We can use our life's advantages or our life's disadvantages to the same degree to bend that light and propel our joy.

In the following chapters, you will find the lessons I discovered through the pursuit of joy. No matter where you are on life's journey, whether sixteen or sixty, unemployed, blue collar, middle manager or executive, I have you covered. I have been all of these at one point on my journey. I've worked in landscaping, as a grocery store clerk, and as a sales coordinator for a company that sold bug zappers. The majority of my career, twenty-nine years of it, was spent steadily working my way up the corporate ladder at Parker Hannifin, an American Fortune 500 company that is one of the largest in motion and control technologies in the world. The company is over a hundred years old, and while you may have never heard of it, there's a good chance you've benefitted from what they make. They manufacture parts for a wide range of applications: medical diagnostic equipment, air conditioners, refrigerators, construction equipment, cars, trains, water purification systems, and parts for planes ranging from Charles Lindbergh's *Spirit of St. Louis* to the US Air Force's F-16s.

I started there as an entry-level management trainee on the factory floor of an automotive division in a little town in Northeast Arkansas. I moved my way up to Global Operations Manager and ultimately became a Division GM running a mini business within a corporation that in 2009 was generating $12 billion in revenue. I've done everything there from clerical work and manual labor, to front line supervisor and quality control, to rescuing plants in Germany and the US and building a plant from scratch in Mexico. Along the way, I learned about teamwork, productivity, and leadership through experience and from many people who came before me and were willing to show me the way through advice and example. Today, I serve as Executive Vice President/COO of the BUNN Corporation, a small family-owned company that has allowed me to continue my growth.

Parts of my resume may look like a charmed life, but there were challenges, obstacles, and a health crisis that threatened to stifle my happiness. Life and career lessons shaped, bent, and sometimes broke me, revealing a new definition and clearer meaning of the pursuit of joy.

While this book is written from my perspective as a business leader, it is for everyone. We are all leaders, and we are all in some kind of business. No matter if you're running a household, a small department, or CEO of a major corporation, it's a business. Whether you realize it or not, you are influencing someone, and someone is following you. It may be kids, friends, or someone admiring you from the shadows. You are making your imprint on someone's life.

It is my desire to take my learnings and combine them with yours to give you a head start or maybe a refocus. We won't make a Hallmark movie out of it where everything in the end is perfect and has a nice tidy bow on it. But together, we can, just like the prism, take your bends, angles, and circumstances to create a beautiful journey. It won't look like mine, and it won't look like your colleague's or your friend's. You are unique. It will be yours. You can make your life joyous.

CHAPTER 1

The Joy of Work–
Making Work Meaningful

"People rarely succeed unless they have fun in what they are doing." –Dale Carnegie

It is estimated that over a lifetime the average person spends 90,000 hours at work. The average American worker spends an additional 100 hours a year commuting. That's a lot of work and work-related time to be either joyful or miserable. Most of which we control.

Too often we associate work with a negative connotation. It's a have-to thing in order to get what we want. Many think of it as how they pay for what they need, or swapping time for the resources to have a little fun. Does that describe you, or someone you know or work with? We've all had negative thoughts pertaining to work. A feeling of dread that seems to paralyze us from time to time. Or maybe it is pure hatred for the type of work, the boss we have, the shift, or just the work in general. How do we capture joy in these circumstances?

As a child, hard work was all around me. It was displayed in front of me daily and became a part of my DNA. My grandfather William Tell Watson, a carpenter by trade, was always tinkering with something. He and my grandmother, Flora Louella, lived a few houses down the block from us and I enjoyed hanging out with them. They were always carpentering, gardening, canning, or something. To us grandkids, they grew everything. It seemed like there was always at least one fruit or veggie in season. One time a guy from our church asked my brother Rick, "what all do they grow in that garden?" He responded, "orange juice and bologna!"

My parents, John L. and Bessie Gay Watson, were two of the hardest working people I've ever known. My mom worked as a janitor most of my life along with all the domestic duties of raising three boys and taking care of my dad's parents and her own mother. I remember my earliest years trying to ride that old Electrolux pull-along tube-style vacuum cleaner as she cleaned the miles of carpet at our church. She eventually got me off that Electrolux and trained me to be a productive cleaning member of the family. My job was to pick up paper on the auditorium floor and in the hymnal racks. I later graduated to my own vacuum–a Kirby upright, thank goodness–and vacuumed the annex of children's classrooms.

As I did my cleaning chores twice weekly on Monday and Thursday, I would always look for faster ways to get my work done or avoid work altogether. I enjoyed having "big boy" jobs, but I'd rather have fun. I had things to do: bikes to ride, swimming at Reynold's Park with my friend Steve, hanging out at the old roundhouse rail yard, hunting with my friend Reggie. Work was something I had to do to get to what I wanted to do. I think in those days I attributed my dissatisfaction to the fact that none of my jobs actually "paid" money. I had learned to work, but I hadn't learned to work joyfully.

I did love the accomplishment of seeing finished jobs. Whether it be a clean building, shucked corn, blackberry preserves, or a completed carpenter project, it was satisfying. What I didn't enjoy was how tired everyone was at the end of the day, or seeing other families go on cool vacations while our vacation was taking a ride "in the hills on a fall day." It seemed that families like ours who worked so hard should get to share in some of these luxuries of life.

I'm not sure how I missed the lesson of working joyfully since my earliest memories are hearing my grandmother singing African American spirituals and my mom whistling as they did their chores. My grandfather somehow managed to keep a permanent smile on his face despite failing health and having to keep up with my grandmother, who had a powerful personality. I wasn't getting it.

My first paying job started in the summer of 1971 when I was twelve years old. I knew Mr. Meadows, a schoolteacher who supplemented his income in the summer doing landscaping and lawn trimming, employed kids occasionally. I asked him at church one Sunday if he could use me. After all, I wanted to be appreciated and paid for my work.

He agreed to take me on for a few hours a week and would pick me up at my house on the mornings I was scheduled to work. I was too cool. Not only was I a productive member of the working community, but I was getting paid as well. I usually worked with my friend Reggie who had hired on with Mr. Meadows the summer before. We did things like rake leaves or trim hedges or pull weeds from flower beds. We would also do the pick-up work after the job was done. We would wind up the electrical cords, sweep, and place all the equipment and ladders back on the truck.

The days were hot, and the work was all manual. The job came with the additional pressure of having to be ready on time and working till whatever Mr. Meadows determined was quitting time. We only took breaks from our work at the appointed time. We were on his schedule. A real working schedule.

My happiness at the time was in making money and I loved being able to tell people I had a real job. That seemed to be enough to motivate me for the first several weeks. I could afford a few luxuries such as an occasional new record album, Dr. Pepper, or a snow cone. But it was still work and it was peculiar how this whole job thing was taking over my life. Far too soon, I started to dread getting up and working in the hot sun. I secretly wished for rain, cooler weather, or for school to start back. I wanted the money; I just didn't like having to work so hard for it. I was already finding that happiness was a slippery state. It easily slid from my grasp as circumstances changed. While the extra income was providing for some niceties, the satisfaction they gave was short-lived. I kept moving the goal line on what I thought would make me happy, which just made me more dissatisfied and unhappy. Does any of this sound familiar? Have you ever worked for something—a car, a promotion, a vacation— only to lose the happiness it brings once you have it?

I found it strange that Mr. Meadows whistled or sang while he worked. He was a male version of my mom and grandmother. Why did these old people do this? He seemed genuinely happy sweating through his khaki work uniforms and safari hat while manicuring yard after yard. Me, I wanted to hurry up, get through the day, and get paid.

Frequently we would drop by his house around break time and his wife Katherine would give us a Dr. Pepper and a snack. I sometimes wondered if she was horrified at bringing two sweaty pre-teens and a husband who'd been working in yards all morning into her clean kitchen. If she minded, she didn't show it. He would remark to her how well we were working, and he wanted to give us a treat. They both were always smiling and seemed to almost be at a giggle when talking. We would have our treat and he would kiss her goodbye. As we loaded back up in the truck for a few more hours of work, he would frequently blurt out, "Whew! You boys stink," and let out a belly laugh as we tooled off down the road to our next assignment.

As we got more comfortable working together, I began asking him a lot of questions. "Why do you do this kind of work? Why do you work so hard? How can you be so happy while dealing with some of these cranky people?" The list went on.

His answers weren't satisfactory for my curious mind. He said he needed something to do in the summertime that kept him active after being in a school room all year. It gave him a chance to do something new. He liked the satisfaction of seeing a completed job done well. He liked to interact with and make people happy.

As an adult, I now see that he wasn't "on the job," he was "in the job." He was throwing himself into his work and making his life and others' lives better every day because of who he was and how well he did it. He was a person who lived from mountaintop to mountaintop and not valley to valley. Valley to valley folks tend to see the worst in their current situation— they hope to get out of it soon, but they're focused on the next potential valley. Mountaintop to mountaintop folks always look from their peak in life to the next expected peak. Sure, they have low points, valleys, but that's not where they're focusing their sight. Regardless of where they are, they know another mountaintop is somewhere in their future, and they live expectantly looking to the next peak. It's the same landscape, it just depends on where you aim your focus.

We all know mountaintop to mountaintop folks, and we all know valley to valley folks. More than likely we have been both for different periods of our lives. Recognizing where we are standing when taking in our views is half the battle of making sure we are getting the right view.

So how do you get this mountaintop perspective and how do you keep it? First, accept you won't always be able to stay at any summit. Second, let's agree that you *can* get there no matter where you are right now. Focusing on mountaintop views rather than valley views is a choice. Sometimes it requires discipline. Sometimes it is a matter of sheer grit.

Early in my career, I had an executive that was trying to motivate our team by seeing the larger purpose in our jobs. His point was that, in our own way, we were doing something important and needed in this world. We made air conditioning parts. Not the complete air conditioners, just specific pieces for them. In our minds, there was nothing sexy or essential to what we did. Our only motivation was making money for ourselves and the corporate machine. It kept us employed. We doubted the world would know or care if we went away.

When the executive heard our response to his big picture challenge, he reset our view. He told an elaborate story about his grandmother and her health risks with heart disease and asthma. She had to have air conditioning to breathe, to live. He talked about how as a teen he depended on her to care for him and raise him since he was orphaned due to a tragic accident. He went into specific detail about how he and his grandfather were dependent on her and how getting air conditioning in their home saved their loved one and made their lives better.

Our work, he said, wasn't welding a joint, cutting metal, or machining a thread. It was much more than that. It was building a better life. A safer life. We were providing comfort to the elderly and sick. We were making hospitals more sanitary. We were making military vehicles that operate in the desert more comfortable and keeping our service men and women safe. We were indeed creating a better life.

To this day, I'm not sure if the executive's story was true or not, but it made an impact on me. How well we do our jobs is in direct correlation to how we see our work and our satisfaction in the job. All work can be viewed from a mountaintop, seen in context as essential and needed. It may require us to adjust our sights and recalibrate our thinking, but it can be done.

Mr. Meadows, my mom, and my grandparents weren't just working to get paid. They were making it part of a joyous life. They whistled and sang while they worked. They saw value in their work and the satisfaction of a job well done. Work wasn't something that held them hostage until retirement. Retirement to them was an added benefit while they continued to work. Work itself was a gift of life and a reward of being healthy. They chose to love every minute of it. Maybe you know people like this in your life too? If so, think about them and how they work.

What is driving them? Are they a mountaintop to mountaintop person? I bet they are.

It doesn't matter how menial you think your job is, someone is depending on you. If you don't show up for work, something eventually doesn't get done. Someone is impacted. We saw this during the Covid pandemic. There were shortages of so many everyday things we usually take for granted—meat, cleaning supplies, personal protective equipment (PPE). It quickly became clear who were essential workers.

Make all your work essential. Find the value and joy in everything you do. Plan how you can take a mountaintop view of your next workday, workweek, and career. You will enjoy your life more fully and will truly find the joy of work.

CHAPTER 2

The Joy of Integrity– Do the Right Thing

"Real integrity is doing the right thing, knowing that nobody's going to know whether you did it or not."
–Oprah Winfrey

I n ethics, integrity is regarded as the honesty and truthfulness or accuracy of one's actions. Wikipedia says integrity is the practice of being honest and showing a consistent and uncompromising adherence to strong moral and ethical principles and values. Definitions like this are found in many corporate mission statements and boardrooms. In a recent assignment of mine, a group used the phrase *honesty, courtesy, and integrity* to describe their desired operating mission. But no matter what is on the wall or printed on paper, it's what's lived out day to day that tells you and others if integrity is present or not. Integrity is like being pregnant. You are or you're not. You have it or you don't. There is no such thing as half pregnant or partial integrity.

My first real world exposure to integrity was as a teenager working part time during high school at Vern Williams' Big Star grocery. The Williams had their 5 to 8 adult workers run the store Monday through Saturday, but the evenings and Sundays were staffed with high school and college kids. Our job was to stock the store during off hours and service the shoppers. There was nothing quite like working for the Williams. It's where I learned most of my curse words, from Vernon AND Lorene! As rough as they could be, they were the salt of the earth. A small-town grocery store, Big Star didn't have a fancy mission statement or code of ethics hanging on a wall. Instead, the family lived their mission from the heart and soul day after day.

The Williams taught me the integrity of work and fair play. In retrospect, it seems strange that Vernon trusted a bunch of teenagers to manage and stock his store at night with no adult supervision. I can only imagine he was teaching us life lessons while at the same time grooming floor managers from the kids that weren't leaving for college.

In my time at Big Star, I remember three events that shaped me forever. The first one happened shortly after I started. It was a busy weekend, and the cry went out over the P.A. "All grocery helpers to the front." That meant lines were forming behind the registers, and sack boys were needed. Vernon hated for customers to wait. He was a customer service freak. He said, "If we don't give them quick service, they will take their business elsewhere."

We managed through the rush with minimal wait times for our customers, but one odd thing happened. Vernon came down from his upstairs office with the two-way mirror and started bagging groceries. Once the crowds had gone, he summoned all the grocery help not on cash registers to the back for a store meeting. We all sat on unstocked paper towel boxes and canned goods. Vernon stood in front of us, visibly angry. He took a moment to compose himself. He then proceeded to tell us that there are all kinds of people in the world. Some good and some not so good. He stressed that as Big Star workers, it was not our place to make that judgement. He said even if it was, he didn't care. He emphatically told us, "Folks, some of these people may not be worth a sh&*, but they are still human and their money's still good."

While I did not witness the exact event that caused his speech, I later was told that some of the workers had not treated one of the customers with respect. It was unclear if it was based on how they looked or their reputation around town. The lesson we learned that day was respect. Respect for everyone.

The second event happened on the Saturday before Thanksgiving, one of the busiest times in the grocery store business when everyone is shopping for family and the big feast to come. This rainy and cold day in 1976 was no exception. The difference this time was that Vernon and Lorene were shopping! I thought, *really? You couldn't find a better time to shop for your own groceries than the busiest day of the year?* They even went through the check-out line with two carts of groceries. I bagged the groceries in those big twenty-pound brown grocery sacks and loaded them back into the cart. Vernon handed me the key to the old white delivery van with an address and directions for delivery. I followed the directions to a road that I didn't even know existed in the most rural part of Greene County.

It was an awkward delivery. He'd told me to make them take the groceries and drive off. When I pulled into the rural remote drive, dogs started barking and someone was peering out the window. I felt more like a bill collector than a grocery delivery guy. A middle-aged lady met me on the porch, but before she could say anything or run me off her property, I announced that I had a food delivery compliments of Vern Williams' Big Star. She had sort of a hurt, embarrassed smile but began taking the bags of groceries from me, placing them inside the door. I quickly said a "Happy Thanksgiving" and drove off without making further eye contact. I never knew who these people were, and Vernon never told me other than to say that everyone should have a good Thanksgiving. The lesson I learned was that in life we must be mindful of those less fortunate.

The third and last event that shaped me at Big Star happened late on a Wednesday evening at store closing. I had been working at the store for about three years, and had earned a promotion to a night manager. Night managers received a more favorable work schedule and more hours, plus a 50-cent-per-hour premium. Our duties included managing the other young workers, making sure the shelves got stocked, waiting on customers, and locking up for the night. Once the store entrance was locked and the building secure, I routinely had the lead cashier open every register and sign off on each. It was a system I'd come up with for the sake of efficiency. The head cashier was to leave the drawers open, so I could pick them up quickly to stack and place in the safe. We were always tired on Wednesday because that was stock night in addition to doing our regular grocery duties. We had a full staff, and everyone was eager to go home. Bowing to pressure, I agreed to let all of them go except one other manager. The two of us scrambled around the store for the next thirty minutes doing lockdown proceedings and hurriedly left.

I went straight home, grabbed a snack, did some homework, and went to bed. About 2:00 a.m., I woke and sat straight up in bed in a cold sweat. I had left every register open with the money still in the drawers. I woke my mom and told her what I had done and that I had to go back to the store. I called the police and had them meet me there so I wouldn't be by myself. I was scared. By 3:00 a.m., I was back in bed with the cash drawers secure in the safe. I knew I'd probably be fired when Vernon found out what a careless and irresponsible mistake I'd made.

I faced it head on the next day and went to his office.

"I guess you heard what happened last night," I sheepishly said. The police officer had said he would have to file a report.

"Do you want to tell me?" Vernon asked.

I said I didn't, but that I had no choice. I proceeded to go through the whole evening. By the time I got to the end of the story, he had a big grin on his face. He admitted he had not heard, but thought I showed a lot of gumption and knew I had now learned a valuable lesson. The lesson I learned was not only to own up to my mistake but also never let efficiency impact the quality and integrity of my work.

Corporate or business integrity is important, but true joy is when we as individuals are known to be true persons of integrity, doing what is right even when we think no one is looking or even notices. It convicts us when we experience it. It inspires us when we witness such an event, especially when the person thinks no one is looking or will ever know.

In my corporate life, I have been fortunate to have been surrounded primarily with people of integrity. Of course, during my time I've seen a few that would cut corners or skirt issues if there was "no harm—no foul." We all know or have worked with this type of person. They are the ones that love to pound on the desk about integrity when it applies to others dealing with them or their company, but when it comes to their own personal behavior, they tend to move toward the letter of the law and abandon the spirit of the law. If you can legally do something but it harms another, that's not integrity. These people usually surround themselves with a legal staff or established set of rules or agreements that benefit them. If someone suffers a misfortune, they are quick to deny any responsibility, saying, "I wish I could help, but that's the rule," or "Sorry, there's nothing I can do, that's the agreement." The truth is they could try to do something, but it would be inconvenient or might cause them difficulties, so they use rules as excuses.

Working for that type of leader has a ripple effect on the whole organization. It becomes an organization built on mistrust and legal agreements. There is no spirit or soul left but instead hollow lifeless people executing on legal transactional agreements. "You pay me, and I will do exactly (to the letter) what you say. Nothing more, nothing less." It's not that the people are bad, they are just disengaged. They do as much as they must and no more. No one wants to work in a legalistic environment that promotes these types of values. Good personal relationships don't work this way and neither do successful companies. Thanks to this soulless leader, this organization or department will be less than successful long term and be life-draining to work for. The environment will be defined by things like high turnover, low morale, back-biting, slow execution, and poor customer service.

The leader of this organization will blame his staff and co-workers for the problems. "If they would do what I say, we wouldn't have these problems." What this leader doesn't understand is, they *are* following orders, the lead, the temperament, and design. To do otherwise would create a moral cramp. It is impossible to demand someone work in the "spirit" of the agreement, if you are going to enforce the "letter" of the agreement. At first it is just the employees that feel this compromised breach of integrity, but soon this trickles down to the customers and this is when things start to crumble.

We all know companies that are known for their customer service, making things right. You know what else they are known for? Integrity. Integrity with their employees and of course their customers.

Last spring, after a long winter and a few health setbacks, my wife Stacie, along with our son Tate, decided to take a trip to the Florida Keys. It is always an adventure traveling or doing anything with our son with Down Syndrome. He's been God's gift to an A Type personality with no patience, my continual reminder that everything doesn't have to happen fast or as planned. I often say that "hurry Tate" is an oxymoron. It's like jumbo shrimp or crash landing. He can add color or flavor to every situation or circumstance.

We booked a flight out of St. Louis on Southwest Airlines. Our itinerary was to go from St. Louis to Austin, Texas; change planes, and continue to Key West. It was a little tight on the plane change, but even with Tate we figured we would be fine. We landed in Austin, gathered our belongings, and headed to our next gate. We had a few minutes, so everyone used the rest-room, and the boarding began. Due to my Type A personality, I paid a little extra for premium boarding. As soon as we took our seats, Stacie asked Tate, "Where's your computer?"

"Whoops," Tate replied. He had left it on the other plane, slid down against the seat and the side of the plane.

"That Mac is gone," I told Tate and Stacie. There was no way we were going to retrieve a computer sitting on another plane going to God knows where with zero identification on the com-puter or the computer sleeve. I was furious to put it mildly.

Still, hoping against hope, I jumped up and headed to the front of the plane to tell the flight attendant what had happened. She asked where the plane had originated and approximately what row our seats were in, then said she would put a call out and see what they could find.

The plane continued boarding with typical Southwest effi-ciency and we all felt sick as the time was ticking away fast. It was a crappy start to a vacation. Tate was miserable knowing he was not going to have his computer all week and maybe never again. I was upset at our ineptitude and the fact that the bill for this vacation had increased by at least another $2,000 bucks. To top it all off, we were all a little snippy at one another.

As the door of the plane was about to close, a breathless Southwest employee came running onto the plane. The flight attendant held up the computer, looking at me and mouthing, "Is this it?" I was dumbfounded. I'm not sure who was happier, us or the flight crew. They were so proud of their work helping to make a family a little less stressed.

Southwest has always strived to demonstrate integrity with both their employees and their customers, and that translates to premiere customer service. Sure, they make mistakes, but they always work to make things right. They were the only airlines during the pandemic to make a promise to their employees there would be no furloughs in 2020 while the rest of the industry shed over 50,000 jobs.

You and I both know that Southwest Airlines is not perfect. We also know that we as individuals aren't 100% perfect. But if we can keep integrity as our centerpiece, we will enjoy the pursuit of our efforts. Just as the joy evidenced on all our faces and the Southwest crew's faces after miraculously producing that laptop, we too can continue and propagate joy by living lives of integrity.

CHAPTER 3

The Joy of Words–
I've Never Regretted Anything
I Didn't Say

(But I've Regretted a Whole Lot of What I Did Say!)

"Whoever keeps his mouth and his tongue keeps himself out of trouble." –Proverbs 21:23 (ESV)

My dad, John L. Watson wasn't a big man. He was reasonably quiet and only 5'9" but he had huge character. Don't get me wrong. He could argue for what he believed in with the best of them. I can remember him and some of his colleagues at church or the school board arguing sometimes to the point I thought they would exchange blows. But when all had been said, they would admit they loved and cared for each other and would agree to disagree. This was peculiar to me.

My dad left this earth too early at the age of fifty-nine with a malignant brain tumor. My family had taken a rare vacation to Washington D.C. along with my middle brother Rick and his wife Lynn. We were in front of John F. Kennedy's gravesite when my dad collapsed with a seizure. He lived another nine months after his diagnosis and surgery. I was in my junior year of high school, so I never got to fully appreciate his character and what truly made him who he was. By worldly standards, his qualifications were few. He had an 11th grade education from Lepanto, Arkansas High School. During WWII, he was classified as 4F in the armed services for flat feet. He spent his life in blue collar jobs. In my lifetime, he was a policeman, managed a gas station, worked at a tire store, was a rural mail carrier, and at the time of his death was serving as the Police Chief for Paragould, Arkansas.

During the time leading up to the funeral and the funeral itself, I remember being bewildered by the fuss that was made at his passing. Of course, we as his family were devastated, but I had no idea that this quiet man had made such a mark on our small community. His funeral was attended by church leaders, local dignitaries, and politicians, and was conducted with the pomp and circumstance of a police funeral. Although I understand this more now, at the time, I thought "who was this man?" I rarely heard him speak. What could explain his impact on this many people from so many different areas of the community?

I really can't remember what the first thing was that I learned as a professional, but I can safely say that learning to be silent in key situations is the best thing I've learned thus far. I am a passionate person. Everything I do is with passion or I won't, or can't, do it. I play with passion, exercise with passion, work with passion, and generally live my life with passion. There's nothing wrong with that per se, but many times I carried it too far or channeled it in very unproductive ways using strong and biting words. I cringe now at how I sometimes behaved in front of family and friends. I sincerely thought my passion and my ability to win the war of words was my best quality. And on some days, maybe it was.

My inability to keep my tongue in check probably carried forward from my teen years. I always admired quick wit and a sharp tongue in others, as long as it wasn't directed at me. I thought it was cool, a sign of intelligence. I consciously and unconsciously worked to be that person. I wanted to "out-talk" the other person—get the last word. I equated this with victory and being the superior mind. I can honestly say that I accomplished this goal and was proud of it. It gave me a certain level of success. As a result of my quick speech, others declared me the winner or let me have my way. I became the de facto spokesperson for a said cause or the leader of the team. This only fueled my misguided trait to greater heights. Be quicker witted. Argue the point with more passion. State that position with more vigor.

I fell victim to this dogmatic behavior early in my career. Passionate and sure that my way must be the best way and best for everyone, I achieved a level of success that allowed me some latitude in getting away with this behavior. My bosses liked my results well enough that they were willing to tolerate some of my brashness during meetings and in my interactions with my peers. In my mind, I was "winning."

I began my career in the early '80s working in manufacturing/operations. After a short stint with an electronics manufacturer, I landed at a plant in a small town in northeast Arkansas in Parker Hannifin's Automotive Connectors Division. As mentioned in the introduction, Parker Hannifin is a global company that manufactures motion and control systems for mobile, industrial, and aerospace markets. Our job was to produce air conditioner plumbing for the automotive market. Our primary customers were GM, Ford, and Chrysler, known at that time as the Big Three.

I was hired in February of 1982, almost a year after completing my undergrad business degree at Harding University. In the early '80s, jobs were hard to find for most everyone, especially college grads with no experience. Inflation and unemployment were high and the two were commonly added together and labeled the misery index. At the time of my hiring, the misery index had fallen from an all-time high of 19.7% to 14.6%. For context, the misery index at the end of 2020, was 8.06%.[1]

My first assignment at the plant was management trainee. This was the lowest managerial position. I was to work in every department and try to learn. The goal and hope were that I would find something that I adapted to well, learn some supervisory/leadership skills, and could fill a needed role sometime in the future should an opening become available. Sure, I had my business degree—or, as the plant team called it, "book smarts"—but I knew nothing about real life business and manufacturing.

I was fortunate during my early career to have some wonderful bosses and peers. My first boss was Big Red, aka Jerry, the Plant Manager at the Parker facility in Trumann, Arkansas. Jerry came by the name Big Red honestly. He had bright red hair, was 6' 4" tall, and easily weighed around 260 pounds. However, the biggest part of Jerry was his heart. Jerry taught me a lot about winning and about relationships. He provided an environment

---

1 "Misery Index by President," United States Misery Index (website), accessed July 16, 2021, http://www.miseryindex.us/indexbyPresident.aspx.

in his plant like none other I had ever experienced. He ran the facility like a family. It was okay for us to fight and argue with each other, but woe be it to anyone on the outside to attack one of us. We would rally around each other and together we were a force to be reckoned with. He usually didn't interfere with our internal skirmishes as long as it was resolved fairly and in short order.

I generally carpooled with a couple of other guys, but if you were offered a free ride home in Big Red's station wagon, it meant he had something serious or confidential he wanted to discuss. I really don't remember my other two coworkers ever receiving such an honor, but I was offered a ride–twice.

The car rides started out pleasant enough. He always had country music playing uncomfortably loud on the radio. He might turn the volume down some, but we still had to talk above the likes of Reba McEntire, Conway Twitty, and George Strait, punctuated by the local crop report and farm commodity price announcement. He'd make small talk and generally affirm my efforts and overall results. Once that was done, he would get to the real reason for the ride–the use of my words. He didn't want to dampen my spirit or my success but wanted me to find a way to get the same results without being brash and hurtful to my peers. He felt if my words were softer or used more to convince, it would improve my leadership and make it more conducive for the team to follow. The goal was positive results that were recognized as a team win and not an individual win where the other members were made to feel like losers. I knew he was right, but it seemed that the heat of the battle and the urgency to produce bottom-line results lessened my resolve to change.

In my twelve years working for Big Red, I also had twelve performance appraisals. I kept every one and still have them today. I always received "exceeds" ratings, and always got chastised in the summary for being too harsh in my comments to my peers. You would think I would have learned.

My quick tongue wasn't helped by one of my best friends in the plant, who may have had a quicker tongue than I did. Russ was funny with his wit, but it could bite. He and another one of our cohorts could swap barbs and quote sayings all day long. When a project was completed, or times were going well we would say, "we're in tall cotton." If we spotted someone wearing baggy clothes, we'd say, "That fits like socks on a rooster." We'd nickname a person "Lightning" or "Speedy" if we thought they were slow in their work or problem-solving pace. Some of these jabs would leave us in stitches, and they weren't intended to be mean-spirited, but they could obviously be more hurtful than we acknowledged to those on the wrong side of it. Of course, not all of our wit was aimed at others. They were funny guys, and I was blessed overall to have them as my friends and coworkers. I remain friends with both today, and they still keep me laughing!

Big Red was the man responsible for putting this group of crazies together. He somehow had the foresight to assemble a winning team that could have fun. To this day, I wonder what he must have told his family and friends about working with all of us.

I was fortunate to follow in Big Red's footsteps upon his retirement. I was a little intimidated but honored, nevertheless. You really want to avoid following someone so successful. It usually never works out. But I remember Jerry being proud it was me taking his place and he would occasionally call to encourage me. We kept in touch over the years until his untimely death. I was honored to speak at his funeral. I was instructed to keep it light and funny, like Big Red would have wanted. That time I got to use my words in a good way.

Later in my career, I was asked to relocate to our Division Corporate office in Memphis, Tennessee, when I was promoted to Global Operations Manager. I had the good fortune of working for our VP/GM, Tom. Tom, like Big Red, also had a nickname. He was fondly known as The Big Guy. Like Big Red, Tom had the knack of putting together winning teams.

The Big Guy assembled teams that were somewhat unconventional by corporate standards. I remember once being labeled as "cowboys" by our German counterparts. We asked them why they called us that and they said, "You know, you come charging in like the cavalry and fire your guns." Believe it or not, I think they were complimenting us.

It was while working for The Big Guy that I finally learned to temper my tongue. Age, maturity, and his strong determination to bridle me but not break me was key. The Big Guy had the ability to have tough conversations with employees and enhance their self-esteem at the same time. I had witnessed him tackling problems and disputes head on with seasoned business executives. There was no dancing around the issue or playing word games. He addressed the problem and never the person. He laid the issue on the table, avoiding a personal attack on ability or character. While the executive may not be happy about the outcome after the discussion, I never witnessed anyone feeling demeaned or devalued after such a meeting. That doesn't mean that he never disciplined or fired anyone. Of course, he did! He was just able to make his point without personally devaluing the other person.

At this juncture in my career, I had recognized that I needed to "grow up," and I had improved, but not enough. I wanted this skill The Big Guy had, but I didn't realize how critical it was or how badly I was still botching it. With my promotion to Global Operations Manager, I was now supervising and interacting with other influential executives. It was like moving from collegiate sports to the pros. I needed to up my game on addressing conflict and resolving issues at the executive level without belittling others. I needed better use of my words.

I was excited about my first performance appraisal from The Big Guy. My numbers were good. I had proven I had good business acumen. I was ready. I was not surprised that he gave me an "exceeds" review and acknowledged all those good things. At the end of the review, there was a place for general comments. It was a way to write things that wouldn't fit in the checkboxes. I remember at this point he took his glasses off, looked me straight in the eye, and again told me good job. He then casually added an appreciation for my passion and willingness to stand up for what I believed in but went on to say I should listen better and let my peers speak before I criticize or shoot down their ideas. I should "keep my gun in my holster a little longer," he said. Little did he know, I took that as a compliment.

Another year passed and it was time once again for my performance appraisal. I was even more excited this time. My metrics were good. I had increased my area of responsibility. By my standards, who wouldn't want me? Once again, as in the year before, he read each section of the review and commented where needed. He bragged on me where I exceeded and gave me pointers in areas I could grow. It was a good review. We finally got to the end at the comment section and he said, "let's finish this at the club over lunch and a round of golf." I was excited! I must have really impressed him this past year to earn lunch *and* a round of golf!

The Big Guy had also invited a few of my peers to join us. I had hit the big time. I imagined we were going to sit around and celebrate me and all my accomplishments. We grabbed a quick lunch and hit the course. The Big Guy said, "ride with me." I was even more pumped. We made small talk as we played the first six holes. On the 7th hole, a par 5, The Big Guy brought up the appraisal again. He again thanked me for a great year but then said the "gun in the holster" was becoming serious. He told me bluntly it was destroying my effectiveness with the team and ruining my reputation at Corporate. Turns out a round of golf was equivalent to a free ride home in the station wagon.

The next eleven holes may have been the longest golf game of my life. I was devastated but thankful at the same time. I clearly didn't see me as everyone else was seeing me. I had some soul searching to do. I had to make amends and find a way to move forward.

In the next twelve months, I made a conscious effort to "keep my gun in my holster." I was determined to listen first, pause, and think carefully before I made any response. I veered away from argumentative behavior in favor of team discussion and problem solving. The key for me was avoiding a rash response. I conscientiously told myself to wait twenty-four hours when possible before engaging in a volatile discussion to better modify my words and articulate my thoughts. I still "drew my gun" too fast on occasion, but differently from before. Once I recognized it, I would make amends. The occurrences got fewer and fewer as the year progressed. My desire to draw my gun didn't go down, but my ability to use restraint was improving. My relationships were also improving. Nothing dramatic, but much better.

During this time, I routinely discussed my progress or failings with a coworker and bike riding buddy. Bill and I lived in the same neighborhood, were both cycling enthusiasts, and would frequently discuss work events on our early morning rides. Maybe I should rephrase that. Generally he would talk, I would listen. I likened riding with Bill to riding in Lance Armstrong's peloton. I figured if I didn't die of a heart attack or pass out from oxygen deprivation by the end of the ride, it must have been a good one. Talking with Bill would let me vent. I could say things to him that I couldn't say to anyone else. I could also get feedback before I engaged my mouth in public. Our relationship proved invaluable as I was genuinely trying to change, and he was helping me navigate the process.

Finally, my third performance appraisal was due. I wasn't nearly as sure of this one as the previous ones. Yes, my numbers were still good, but it was that blasted comment section I had to deal with. Had I really improved in keeping my gun in my holster? Were the relationships with my peers better? I was about to find out. As before, I was summoned to The Big Guy's office by our admin, Susie. She always gave me 'the look' right before I went in to give me an indication of whether it was good news or bad. This time I was unable to read anything. Crap! What did that mean?

He began as always by reading the check box section first. All good marks and even a couple of outstandings. He seemed to take forever getting through the thing by making one comment after another. He never missed an opportunity to point out growth areas and congratulate me on new milestones achieved. Then, finally, we got to the dreaded comments section. He studied what he had written for a minute, pulled his glasses off, and looked me right in the eye. "I think you are finally getting it!" he said. "You aren't great, but you have shown improvement. My suggestion to you now is throw that d@*n gun away!" He belly-laughed as only The Big Guy could.

It was the best career advice I've ever received. I mean really, why do you need a "gun" anyway? What good was it really doing? It was a personality flaw. It was hampering my ability to build relationships based on trust. It was also ruining my ability to build consensus on critical issues and strategy.

I had been given a golden nugget that would serve me well for the remainder of my career. Of course, I still falter every now and again, but it's not my trajectory anymore. That's not who I am. I live by the saying, "I never regretted anything I didn't say, but I've regretted a whole lot of what I did!"

CHAPTER 4

The Joy of Teamwork–
Mediocre or Misplaced?

"Ability is what you're capable of doing. Motivation determines what you do. Attitude determines how well you do it." –Lou Holtz

I love sayings from anyone who is "in the game." I don't care if it's sports, business, medicine, military, manufacturing, or whatever. The key is, they must be someone with a "pound of flesh" to lose just from playing. People in the game can develop sayings and analogies like none other, words of wisdom thought up on the battlefield or because of being in the struggle. Non-players can't make the same impactful statements, no matter how good they are. Until you face the beast eye to eye, you really have never met nor understood it.

That's why I like quotes from notable coaches like Nick Saban, Lou Holtz, and others. No matter if you like them or their team, you know their battlefield quotes will likely apply to your battle at one point or another. I am in no way a Nick Saban and Alabama Crimson Tide fan. I'm an Arkansas boy and always root for Arkansas State University or the University of Arkansas and anyone who plays against Alabama. Respecting an opponent is a whole different thing. I *respect* Alabama, but Arkansas is my home.

So, when Nick Saban said, "High achievers can't stand mediocre people and mediocre people can't stand high achievers," I got it. Coach Saban was obviously referring to football, but it applies to all vocations, teams, and organizations. The tension between the high achiever and the mediocre can limit and even cripple a team in both sports and business.

A few years ago, I had the good fortune of working with an organization development group out of the United Kingdom. I didn't have their skills and credentials, but I did know the team they were hired to consult with. The manager of the team had contacted the consulting group because of what he felt were some execution failures from his team. Due to a recent reorganization, he had inherited a few new/different team members that had changed the dynamics of his original team. Even though individually they had all been successful managers, collectively the job wasn't getting done. There were stalemates, political infighting, and general all-around ill will. Because of this, he wanted to know as a manager, what was he to do? Did he need to change the way he was managing, or did he need to change or rearrange the team?

Part of my role was to place every team member into a four-quadrant personality and leadership profile using a series of profile questions. Analytical was the top left quadrant, and Driver the top right. The top two groups were also categorized as Thinker. The bottom two quadrants were Feeler and were represented as Amiable on the left and Expressive on the right. The left two quadrants (Analytical and Amiable) were grouped as Introvert while the right two quadrants (Driver and Expressive) were Extrovert.

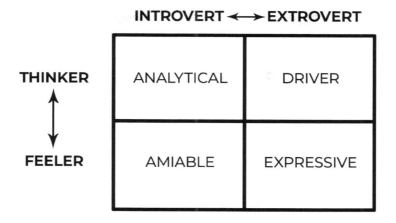

Where a participant was placed in each of the quadrants suggested both a leadership style and how their personality was displayed as a part of that style. If a person was placed in the Driver quadrant, you then had to decide how Extroverted or how much of a Thinker they were. Through my recommendations, they were going to group one team destined for failure and another stacked for success.

The consultant reviewed the individuals and ratings I had given for a little over a half hour and was then ready to place them in groups. Since I knew all the team members, I could start to see a pattern to their grouping. I remember thinking that a fight could break out or worse on the team chosen for failure, and I wasn't totally sure what was going to make the stacked team that successful. Each team had successful members, but the individuals were all so very different in so many ways.

It wasn't that the stacked team had all the same type personalities or a track record of huge leadership accomplishments. But what they did have was a common commitment to excellence. A commitment to completion. A commitment to not failing . . . not permanently failing anyway. They had a balance and diversity of thoughts and ideas. Maybe that was enough.

What did the consultant see in my profiles that allowed him to "pick" a team designed for failure? I remember thinking they were "different" but not sure how to put my finger on the traits that were going to destine them to defeat. No doubt the consultant could write a book of his own just on the two teams and their profiles explaining it all. To me, there were a lot of differences between the dysfunctional team and the success team, but there were a lot of common traits as well. To me, the most interesting part was watching how each of the teams worked together.

The lead consultant gave each team an identical assignment, rules, and time limit in which to work. The assignment was taken from an actual situation the team was currently facing so it had a realistic feel and urgency to it. Each team was given a flip chart to make a presentation on their findings at the end of the time limit.

The consultant sent each team to a different corner of a large meeting room with chairs and worktables, and we were able to observe from a mezzanine that surrounded the upper perimeter of the room. Once the clock was started, the two teams began their work. Watching from the mezzanine was an experience that I would never forget. It was like an out-of-body experience, as if I were almost watching myself work. I could mentally project myself into their situation because I too had been in similar problem-solving situations almost daily. Not only could I walk around and hear the two teams, but I could watch the teams and their body language. I could see them function on both a macro and micro level.

As I walked around the mezzanine, the team stacked for success was focused and buzzing with ideas and organization. Even though they were predetermined to succeed, they had lively conversation and some disagreements. But they let the clock keep them focused on solving the differences in the interest of time and completing the assignment. While it was obvious they weren't best friends and probably wouldn't even socialize outside this assignment, they were still cohesive and seemed to click. They were also hugely supportive and excited about their accomplishment. In a few short minutes, they had gelled as a team and were ready to present their solution.

In contrast, the team destined for difficulty had intermittent communication and seemed to lack focus and direction. Their first task of choosing a leader was painful to watch. The members that wanted leadership couldn't garner support while some wanted no part of the leadership position. Many on the team were red faced and frustrated while others seemed to have checked out to focus more on the afternoon's planned golf outing. They tended to break into camps, argue, and end in complacency. The time limit running out only seemed to make the dysfunctional behaviors more pronounced.

When time expired, the dysfunctional team looked to the consultant as if they had been victims. They blamed one another and made excuses. Most of all they had a completely unused flip chart. Nothing was on it. They pleaded for more time. There was no end to the excuses.

The consultant dismissed the other team for a break and told the dysfunctional team they could have another fifteen minutes, but they had to spend that time getting their action plan on the flip chart, choose a presenter, and make their case for their recommendation.

The next fifteen minutes may have been more painful than the original session. Time was now an even bigger enemy. The team was more agitated and even more focused on blame. The one chosen to write on the flip chart started and stopped at least a half dozen times and would end up tearing off and wadding up another page. In the interest of time, instead of listening to the team bicker, she finally started writing her own list. In all fairness to her, she did a pretty good job coalescing the team's thoughts into a manageable action plan while the rest of the team continued to argue with one another.

After the break, it was time for each team to present their findings. The contrast between the two teams was quite remarkable. The team destined for failure went first. The presentation was choppy and disjointed. Disagreements were made known, and the first action item wasn't actually an action but rather a study and evaluation of the problem. The actions they did have weren't concise and lacked full team commitment. It was clear the team didn't want to be held responsible for the results. They eventually finished after more coaching from the consultant and then sat in silence with their arms crossed on their chests–distancing themselves from the assignment and their fellow team members.

When the team destined for success started presenting, they were excited. Their thoughts were organized and convincing.

They had a unity to their tone. The presentation was smooth with members interjecting at the right times, providing clarification and support. Even the dysfunctional team was jumping in and affirming the other team's thoughts. It was something right out of a management textbook. It seemed staged and surreal.

Was the dysfunctional team made up of bad employees? No. Was it a bad mix of employees? Yes. Every one of the employees on both teams went on to continue successful careers, some in their current role and others with a different company or position. Were some of these employees "mediocre?" Maybe . . . at least in their current role. Or maybe the issue was like what Nick Saban said, a clash between the high achievers and the mediocre.

Coach Saban doesn't have time to counsel his "employees" or switch their role within the "company;" the time span of a football season is short. If you don't turn in a winning season in Alabama, you don't last long. Even a winning season without a national championship will be short-lived. In this country, we value sports more than real life. Sad, but true. In Coach Saban's viewpoint, you are there to produce 100% or you are out. Outside the Nick Saban world, this tends to not be so urgent. I have found that many organizations survive with mediocrity and poorly formed teams with no awareness of their shortcomings and seem to be proud of it. Some will boast they aren't like those "cut-throat" organizations that are always looking to eliminate their bottom performers. Instead they are of the illusion that they are making their organization better by grooming the bottom 10%.

Let's think about that for a minute. As an organization, they are going to focus and invest time and money on the bottom performers. The flip side of that means devoting fewer resources to the top performers and the 80% in the middle that are getting the job done day after day. Then they wonder why they can't keep their top fliers and lose a good portion of their doers to other companies or by allowing them to slip back into low performers.

I have never heard a Top 20 coach at a press conference after the game talk about bringing up the bottom of their roster to the middle. Coaches like Nick Saban succeed year after year by focusing on the top of their roster, not the bottom. Yet, as crazy as it sounds, there are organizations that do this by default every day. All their policies, efforts, and management systems are geared around the low performers while the workhorses and top performers get nothing. This type of system will get you the best mediocre team money can buy. If that's working for you, so be it. Just don't be surprised when your organization can't compete, or it becomes irrelevant.

The process of getting the right team in place can be painful but necessary for the success of both the individual and the organization. To do nothing is not an option if you want to win. Doing nothing is guaranteed to make the high performers leave, leaving you with nothing but the mediocre and low performers.

In my own leadership experiences, I've found adjusting an existing team is more of a challenge than creating a good team from scratch when you have the freedom to select either new or proven talent. Even if a wrong choice is made, you can adjust without causing a lot of ill feelings since little time has lapsed and tenure in the position is not a factor. (I'll cover team building in more detail in the next chapter.)

When being placed into the leadership position of an existing team, the dynamics change. There are always those long-term tenured employees that stake out their position based on longevity. That could be a red flag on its own, but in some cases great employees tend to play the seniority card before the qualification card. No matter their tenure, as the leader, you must assemble a winning team. To fail to do so is a failure for you personally and for the rest of the organization.

Winning teams that are craftily selected and groomed take on a different air. The whole climate changes when they enter the field of play. They win because they share the joy of hard work. The joy of discipline. The joy of teamwork. On the flip side, we see losing teams with a few bright stars but no team cohesiveness. They tend to focus on blame, injuries, poor individual play, circumstances, and the list goes on. They can win and do occasionally. That's the rub. The problem is they rarely win joyfully.

If you are like me, you can look back on teams you've been a part of that were successful and some that were not. What role did you play? Were you a good fit? If you've been fortunate to be on a strong team, think about why it was that way. Let's use the things we've learned to create the best team possible. But don't stop there, keep reimagining the team. Teams like growth. Strong teams like to win.

CHAPTER 5

The Joy of Building Teams—Select and Rearrange

"Teamwork makes the dream work." –John C. Maxwell

In my thirty-plus years in business, I've only had one occasion where I got to select a team from scratch. My first experience assembling an executive leadership team was an expat assignment to start a plant in Monterrey, Mexico. I had two years to hire and meld a fully sufficient and independent team.

I was short on experience and international savvy so I, along with some key corporate staff, began the interview process by renting space from one of our sister companies in the area to conduct interviews. We ran ads in newspapers and various other publications that we were looking for these individuals for our staff.

We began by looking for a Human Resource manager first. This would be a critical position for hiring and assimilation of the other staff, as well as setting the tone for the other hires. I believe most managers want to uphold good business and moral principles, but sometimes directions can get clouded by stress, competition, and less than clear circumstances that cause the right decision to be less obvious. A great HR manager centered on integrity and grounded with a good moral compass will ensure the long-term success of the organization.

My executive manager and I were in one room, the corporate HR manager and another staff member were in the other rooms. The corporate staff's primary responsibility was to interview the person on competencies, determine if they had the skills, and ask technical questions (how do you hire people? how do you select people?). We had to put together a team based on interpersonal relationships as well as technical skills. As this was the first hire, my key factors were whether this was someone I could work with, and if the person projected the type of atmosphere that I wanted to project. I had the veto power, so to speak, so that though someone may be technically sound, if it wasn't someone I could work with they received a thumbs down, or at best a maybe.

We had some great candidates—professional resume builders with impressive experience and a great success story. It was common at this time for people to over-inflate their qualifications and accomplishments. So, just reading their resumes made it hard to make candidate selections. We eventually decided on Luis for the HR manager position because he had more than a good resume. His personality was a good fit and he was both bilingual and bicultural. He could not only translate English to Spanish and vice versa, he was able to translate both cultures to both parties. For an international company, being bicultural, in my opinion, was as important, if not the most important quality my HR person could have.

Before this opportunity, I had worked in Germany where it was very hard to communicate more than just facts. We weren't that adept at their culture, and they weren't that familiar with ours. When we arrived, the Germans' paradigm of me and my U.S. counterparts was based on our popular culture and movies. They thought we were all cowboys. They said, "we thought you all owned guns and went around shooting things." Talk about a difficult starting position for an assignment. All my new teammates thought I had a gun . . . and would use it.

You must understand where each culture is coming from and what their values are in that culture. That's what struck me about Luis. He could joke in English—political jokes about the situations going on in the US at the time. He could translate political jokes going on in Mexico. We understood more about their culture, and we understood what he and the Mexicans believed about our culture. That trait was imperative not only to the mechanics of what our business was about but also our corporate philosophy and approach to business. Luis stayed with me throughout my time in Mexico and we became great friends.

Our next team member was the Plant Manager, Gerardo. Luis was involved in the interview and hiring of that position. Then we started using their contacts and influence to fill the other positions. As Luis and Gerardo interfaced with each other, we could see the positive team dynamic growing. It was exciting to watch. We gradually hired all the staff—engineering manager, quality manager, plant controller—by relying on each other's contacts and discernment. We learned from each other. The advantage that I had in filling one position at a time was that I could choose for competence, chemistry, and fit as the team expanded. This meant the interviews took several weeks instead of the one week we anticipated—and I hadn't yet relocated to Mexico to work with the staff on a day-to-day basis. But I knew taking the time necessary was important. If properly fitted, the team would draw energy from one another.

It wasn't all perfect. We had a couple people drop out after the first few months. But even with some turnover, we continued to use the same principles to recruit and assimilate new team members. The little turnover we had made us stronger. We were growing and maturing at the same time. The team would stay intact for several years after I left.

We needed a strictly high-performance team in Monterrey. We had deadlines that we were bound and determined to meet. The weaker leaders tended to get left behind and frustrated in that environment. They defaulted to talking about less tangible things or solely focused on getting through the day. They weren't bad employees. They would do anything you asked, but they could get crushed at the pace in which we were moving. To prevent this, they would organically reassimilate somewhere else in the organization where they could be more effective or, in rare cases, they chose to leave the organization to do something more in line with their talent or liking.

Of course, most times you don't get the opportunity to put together your own team. You start with an environment that already exists. My next opportunity was exactly that. I was stepping into a leadership role where the team was already in place at a facility in Trumann, Arkansas. In fact, it was the facility where I had originally been hired. I was coming home. I knew these folks and the dynamics of this process would be very different from what I had experienced in Mexico and proved to be much more challenging. Not only was the team almost complete, with a few exceptions due to retirement or attrition, but I had worked with some of them prior to leaving for Mexico, and now I was the leader.

So, where do you start when *you* are the one joining the team as the leader? It feels very awkward. If it has been a successful team, they may feel no change is necessary. As the leader, you may agree. If they haven't reached a viable level of success, there may be a little room here. In this case, the team had been wildly successful in years past but had recently fallen on hard times. Financial pressure on multiple fronts—a sluggish economy, competition from low-cost countries, and the increasing cost pressures of the automotive industry of the early '90s—had put them in the red and on the verge of shutting their doors.

The Big Guy had sent me to Trumann as caretaker saying, "do your best, but it looks like we will have to 'whack' it." "Whack it" was The Big Guy's term for dealing with all unpleasantries of closing a plant, including firings. I had worked to "fix" a manufacturing plant a few years prior in Germany. I had built a new plant in Mexico. But I had never had to close a plant. I was a wreck. It was MY plant on top of that. I knew these people. I knew their spouses, kids, and parents. I knew the local leaders and other business professionals. This was personal.

And yet it was my job to make sure we were hitting on all cylinders and at maximum output in order to minimize the losses and protect the customer from disruptions as we worked to wind down the operation. That's what it meant when the "whack" word came out. But The Big Guy had prefaced it with *"looks like we will have to"* and also said I was to *"do my best."* In my mind of "better to ask forgiveness than permission," I was free to at least try and save it. Maybe? Somehow.

I had barely settled into my new office before everyone was asking me if I was sent there to close the place. Even they knew the losses had to stop soon. I really didn't know how to respond. I couldn't tell them what The Big Guy had told me: "whack it!" If I did, all the good employees would leave, and I would be left in a pile of rubble, unable to accomplish anything. The survival of this facility would require a different leadership dynamic and new thinking. I also had to decide if it could be done with the existing team, or if a new team would have to be formed.

As I mentioned, this team had been successful in the past. The problem with success is people tend to want to replicate whatever recipe was used to achieve that success over and over, no matter the times or the circumstances. We are all wired this way. It's conditioning. If a certain behavior or behaviors have equated to good things happening, why wouldn't you keep repeating the same things that got you there the first time? But continued success means you often have to evolve and make changes as the world around you changes.

Trumann had more than its share of good common-sense workers, and I've always found the common sense of good ol' Arkansas folks refreshing. This made the job much easier and moved it along a lot faster. But no matter how smart or how much common sense they possessed, as with any normal distribution of population, there were still team issues and misfits within the team. Sometimes they would work themselves out. Sometimes they would not and I had to address it.

As we began to fill open positions in the Trumann team, the high performing members started making their mark. They were setting lofty goals and achieving them in short order. A gap began to grow between the high performers and those perceived as less capable. We had some departments excelling while others seemed to lag ever further behind, resulting in backbiting and team dysfunction. Some of it was a healthy tension while some was just toxic frustration. It quickly became my job to solve this dilemma or I would either lose both groups or force the team into mediocrity and failure.

To complicate matters, I was enrolled in graduate school to work on my MBA at Arkansas State University. I routinely left work after a long day to head straight to class for several hours, go home, have family time, do homework, and like Bill Murray in *Groundhog Day*, do it all over again the next day. It was a vicious and exhausting cycle. But just as Bill Murray would learn a little something every day, I too would learn something daily and advance a little further.

One such day I was introduced to Robert Fisher. Bob retired in 2021 after serving as the President of Belmont University in Nashville, Tennessee for over twenty years. Before that, when we met, he was Vice President of Academic Affairs at ASU and had co-written a book with Bo Thomas called *Real Dream Teams*. At the time of its publication, the phrase "dream team" had been associated with the 1992 US Olympic Basketball team. This team consisted of the greats like Michael Jordan, Charles Barkley, Scottie Pippen, and others. The book calls this *dream talent* and not dream team. The dream teams that Bob and Bo wrote about had to do with assembling good talent and making the team great. This was exactly what I needed to learn how to do. What we really had was mediocre to good talent but extraordinary heart and work ethic.

Bob agreed to consult with our team and do some training off-site on weekends. We all read the book *Real Dream Teams* and were excited about our possibilities. By worldly standards, no one would pick us as a team. Few of us were polished professionals. We had varying degrees of education, wide age range, and varied backgrounds. Our team consisted of some local good ol' boys, a couple of recent college engineering grads, and a couple of corporate recruits who were the only trained and educated professionals we had. Except for Hal, my HR Manager and lifelong childhood friend that I recruited on my return to the plant, this was the team that was in the building when I got there. Sure, I did some rearranging and assignment changes, but ultimately this was the starting line-up.

Bob spent many painful hours going through exercises and teaching us how to get along, work together, and create a common purpose. Most of all he taught us first how to be a team, win or lose, and then how to become stronger as a team. Then all we had to do was work together to figure out how to not get "whacked."

We completed our time with Bob and formulated a management game plan for how we would each work individually and how we work with each other. We were on our way. We had a few slip-ups now and then due to big personalities, but ultimately, we would remember our guiding principles and the personality would yield for the good of the team.

To further our team's growth, we bought dozens of copies of small, easy-to-read manufacturing books by authors such as Ken Blanchard and Sydney Sheldon. We offered these books to anyone who wanted to read them, from the salary staff and production line workers to the engineering and drafting teams. These were books to help us make teams throughout our ranks and to allow hourly and salary associates to share goals and sameness of vision.

On Fridays at our production meeting, each of the supervisors would take turns discussing what they learned in each of the chapters and how they could be applied throughout the company. One of our main champions was a veteran production supervisor, James. He was always eager to learn and was more than happy to discuss. James would talk frankly about his own mistakes and shortcomings. He was helping to create an open environment and a safe place to discuss new viewpoints. It was through his leadership that many of the other production supervisors jumped on board quickly.

Things were better. We were functioning as a team throughout the ranks. We decided to make a declaration day that would announce to the world our intentions going forward. We called it "Make It Happen Day." We had t-shirts printed, coffee mugs, signs, and all sorts of promotional material. We invited our corporate staff to visit and see our progress. We had a huge "Make It Happen" sheet cake and refreshments for everyone. Even the local TV media got wind of it and wanted to come see what we were doing.

The day was a success, as promotional days go, and a boost to morale. But we still had a lot more work to do. We had cut our losses through sheer budget control and better teamwork but losing less was not a recipe for keeping a plant open. It was going to take something revolutionary to make that happen.

Hal, my HR Manager was invaluable in helping to solve this problem. He felt we had made improvements in the management team and now it was time to integrate the team concept into our hourly associates. He introduced one of the scariest concepts I had ever heard at this point in my career: self-directed work teams. I thought *self-directed*? I don't think so. I'm going to direct the teams and they are going to run as I direct. Left alone, they will be directing themselves to longer lunches, longer breaks, and reduced work hours. At least, these were my thoughts until Hal began to train me and my management team about the benefits of self-directed teams and how they work. After several sessions and discussions, we agreed to give it a pilot run in a small area of the plant. We trained the work group and each of us agreed to work and support the roles as we had been taught.

While there are whole books written about self-directed teams, Hal focused on how the teams interact and provide feedback. They were to work as mini businesses by establishing their work and performance goals in alignment with the plant overall goals. They were to decide how work got done and provide feedback to management on problems and opportunities. They were trained and empowered to make changes within their workgroups. The key point we learned from this process was the need to place our performers according to their ability and desire. This benefited the employee and their peers and the overall company performance as well. We were beginning to realize that high performers were more a function of fit and arrangement and less on their innate abilities. Sure, we had stars, but we discovered underperformance was more a fit and placement problem.

The pilot program ran so well that we incorporated this throughout the rest of the plant over the next several months. It caught on like a dry grass fire. Once one department implemented it, the adjacent department would be clamoring for it. They too wanted to have a say in how work got done.

Were there problems? Sure. But here were the keys we used to implement the teams successfully:

1. *Carry the wounded and shoot the stragglers.* That sounds mean and tough, but it really wasn't at all. What we were really saying is if any member wanted to participate and give it a try, we were committed to them to make it work. We would adapt their assignment, change their work, retrain, and do whatever it took to make them successful in the new environment. If they chose not to participate, they were given the opportunity to move to a single contributor role outside of an assembly line or team work cell, such as running a punch press or warehouse stocking where they could basically work alone.

2. *Maintain self-esteem.* We needed everyone. We valued everyone. We worked every day to make sure they all knew that. We had daily, weekly, and monthly team meetings with various management personnel using a white board. Every issue was logged down and addressed at the next team meeting.

3. *Expectation of success.* In the voice of Star Wars' Yoda, "Do or do not, there is no try." We clearly communicated that success was the only option. We would discover how to make that happen.

4. *Openly recognize success and failure–and know failure is temporary.* We gave out small tokens for success–sausage biscuits, popsicles, or t-shirts. Sometimes rewards were plantwide meals and celebrations. Failures were openly recognized and visible on team dashboards. The teams kept a running journal on progress and countermeasures addressing the failures. Today's failure became tomorrow's opportunity.

Teams and team building are a never-ending quest. Once built, they must continually be assessed, tweaked, and re-built. What I and my teams learned was the continual process was the real joy. The joy was in the pursuit. The joy was in continually making it better. They were growing themselves along with their teammates. Dream teams can and should be a reality.

The real proof that we had established dynamic teams was when we would see team members reassign themselves or talk candidly to other team members about their assignment and roles. You could see a spark of pride and accomplishment in their eyes and in the way the team members conducted themselves. They were engaged. They had bought in. They were joyfully part of a team.

We all grew. We grew individually, but more importantly, we grew as a team, numerically and professionally. We grew from each other. As one member improved, it seemed to springboard others to new levels. We continued to work hard but mostly with our brains. We continued to have challenges, but nothing that could steal our joy permanently. There truly was joy in building a team.

CHAPTER 6

The Joy of Efficiency–
I'm Just Lazy Enough to Be
Efficient

"Give me six hours to chop down a tree, and I will spend the first four sharpening the axe." –Abraham Lincoln

S ometimes when I say, "I'm just lazy enough to be efficient" it alarms people. I mean after all who wants to be considered lazy? No one. Me neither. But when you look at what I'm really saying here it is not about laziness. It's about efficiency. I want the luxury of enjoying laziness enough to be efficient and make time for it. I've learned that putting in more time doesn't always lead to better results. Sometimes it's based more on how you go about the work.

Like most parents, when I was a young adult with two kids, I was extremely busy and overcommitted. After a typical full workday there were chamber or civic club meetings, church activities, playing intramural sports, and coaching the kids' seasonal sports. My mom used to comment that doing so much stuff was going to kill me at an early age. My response was, "at least I'll be done." She really didn't *see* me do the work. She thought since I was involved in a lot of things or a lot of things were getting done, that I must be killing myself with being involved in all these activities while working.

It's true that I probably did do too much and was involved in too much. But, even at an early age, I was learning that efficiency was key to getting a lot of things done. And getting a lot done to me equated to a better life and more happiness.

I learned through experiences. As a kid, getting my cleaning chores done more quickly meant I had more time for play, riding bikes, swimming, or hanging out with friends. This is why I became obsessed with efficiency. Less time spent working and more time spent playing. More output for less input. Work smarter instead of harder for the same or more money. Sometimes my efficiency measures back in those days looked like shortcuts that were more about speed and were not always appreciated. But nonetheless I kept trying. I would analyze every chore as I would do it and try to think of ways to make it faster, easier, better.

This efficiency obsession stayed with me through my teen and college years in the various jobs I had working my way through school. Unfortunately, most of my ideas just made me work harder by working faster and not always smarter. Sure, I got the job done and usually done well but not without a few consequences and sometimes increased work. My employers always liked my results and rewarded me accordingly, but it was still not the lift I was looking for.

My obsession with efficiency continued into early adulthood in both work and play. I loved to play sports. I loved to compete even though I was never great at anything I played. I would try any sport if you gave me a challenge. This happened one

Sunday at church when I was challenged by one of the members to run the Monroe 5K. Ethan was a runner before running became cool. He was out running every day, rain, sleet, or snow. He made this awful breathing sound that was his trademark. Ethan had about thirty years on me and was considered by most to be eccentric for his peculiar obsession. The race was a couple of months away, and I figured I had time to train and put this old man in his place. I intended to show him running was no sport for men—it was for all those that couldn't do anything else.

I started training at the track behind my alma mater, Crowley's Ridge Academy. I would drive my big old powder blue 1979 Ford F150 back behind the building right up to the track and start running. Occasionally I would invite my wife Stacie and my son Jared to come watch and marvel at my progress. Over the course of a couple of months, I trained myself to complete twelve laps without stopping. I figured I was ready. No sixty-year-old man was going to top that.

Race day came and like a true rookie, I moved to the front at the start line. I wanted Ethan to only see my backside. I would wait on him at the finish line. The gun went off and I took off as if I was running the 100-yard dash. Before we even got to the first mile marker, I knew I had started too fast. But not to worry, I would slow, recoup, and still whip his butt. As I slowed, I heard that trademark awful breathing sound and watched Ethan pass me with little to no effort. I took off after him thinking I would wear him down. No sixty-year-old can be stronger than a thirty-year-old.

I was wrong. Ethan finished the race so far ahead of me that he crossed the finish line, got water, and then ran back to meet me and finish with me. Humiliating, to be sure, but I was hooked. How can a man this much my elder be more efficient at covering 3.1 miles than me? I was stronger, younger, better built and yet somehow he was faster and fitter.

I soon became a student of running. I read everything I could on the topic. I practiced every trick I could find. Ethan had mastered a Zen-like training style that kept the heart rate slower by limiting unnecessary movement or excitement. Even though his body was working, it was limiting effort through focus and energy preservation.

I trained with Ethan every weekend and would quiz him for ideas on nutrition and strategy. We were soon swapping articles and training tips. We went to weekend races together and became running partners. He was my Mr. Miyagi and I, his Daniel-san.

We continued in this vein with him honing my skills and pushing me to races with greater distances. At first it was 5Ks (about 3 miles), until I owned every local 5K running shirt. He then stretched me to do 10Ks and expanded our geographical coverage. We also added a couple more junior runners to our weekend running crew. We would swap running stories and plan our next race together. Ethan enjoyed the company even though he rarely talked during the runs (something I should have picked up on). He would always say at the beginning of the run, "If someone wants to talk, I will be glad to listen." We were somewhat odd bedfellows, but it was fun.

I knew Ethan ran marathons, but I blocked that notion out of my head. Running twenty-six miles in one stretch was for crazy people. When he would run with me on the weekends, he was doing his "short run" and would reserve the other weekend day for his long training run in preparation for his next marathon. He would always invite me to join him on those marathon runs, but though intrigued, I would politely decline. He would still challenge me to come run as far as I could and cut off at any point to head home.

These invitations went on for the better part of a year before I finally agreed to at least come *start* the run with him. We began at a modest pace, and I was proud of what I could do. He was scheduled to run fifteen miles, and I made it to about mile eight before I stopped. We continued this arrangement for several more months. What Ethan didn't know is that he had me hooked. I wanted to do a marathon, but I needed to be asked. I needed help. This efficiency conundrum concerning running seemed to somewhat level the playing field of age and genetics. The order of finishers didn't necessarily come in by the youngest or most fit in appearance.

After months of doing training runs, Ethan finally invited me to run a marathon with him and some of his elite running friends. I was excited, but scared and unsure at first. I didn't want to look desperate, but I told him I needed help and support. He agreed to help and proceeded to give me several articles and a book on running. I scoured the information and began applying as much of it as I could manage.

After months of training and studying, it was finally time. We all headed to Memphis for the First Tennessee Memphis Marathon. The race was the following day, Sunday, December 6, 1992. The temperature was supposed to start out at a cool forty-three degrees, then warm a little before a rainy cold front passed through. For the elite finishers, this would be no problem. For the three-hours-plus guys, it could be an issue. Ethan finished in three hours and some change while I got to enjoy another thirty-seven minutes beyond that in a driving cold rain. I was still hooked.

I went on to complete about a dozen marathons over as many years. I studied marathons as much as I ran them. I read everything that runners and writers had to say about training and running—breathing efficiency, training efficiency, recovery efficiency, leg efficiency—the whole process. What were the best doing differently than the average runner? What efficiency techniques had they learned that made them better? It all intrigued me.

The obsession with efficiency has always been an integral part of my professional life as well. In business, it is really the most significant measure of health we have. It all boils down to how efficiently we can turn a good or service into a quality saleable product at a profit. Wall Street benchmarks companies by industry and rates them in a measure called revenue per employee. Higher revenue per employee in each industry is one of the components to getting rewarded with a better stock price if all other health data are comparable. This means you are working smarter, not harder.

This leads to a tendency for companies and leaders to ask employees to work harder or chase cheap labor to boost their efficiency numbers. They strive to offshore everything in hopes of making their profit and financial numbers look good. But in most cases, unless something fundamentally changes, this is a shoddy fix that must be repeated time and time again.

True efficiency comes from re-thinking the processes, re-thinking the value proposition.

This was the conundrum we faced in the Trumann plant. Sure, we had formed self-directed work teams and we *had* gotten better. We had cut our losses, productivity was up, and we were finding joy in working the process. But even with those improvements, the pressure from foreign competition and the threat of cancelled contracts were keeping our selling price too low for a comfortable profit margin.

Contracts with automotive companies are of little security. They are written with very little room for the supplier but a lot of leeway for the customer. As much as we would try to put language in place to protect us, if we got too picky, they would move on to the next supplier, leaving us with nothing. Even in the rare case where we might try to enforce a contract by taking them to court, winning against an automotive company in a Michigan court where the contracts usually stipulate matters will be settled, is rare.

The result was that customers would routinely threaten to cancel a contract if we couldn't reduce the price by a targeted percentage. If we gave in, we either reduced profits or worse, lost money. If we didn't give in, we could lose the business and face layoffs and more profit problems. It was a no-win situation.

Despite increased price pressures and contract threats, we continued with our self-directed work teams. We made other incremental improvements. I knew we had some new business coming if we could hold on, and maybe that would improve our margin. But would it all be good and fast enough to prevent "the whack" that was hanging over our heads? I needed answers.

One of the first calls I made was to our controller, Roger. I knew he would tell it to me straight. Thankfully Roger didn't go into the field of medicine because his bedside manner was nonexistent. When I asked what he thought about the plant's financial picture, he promptly responded, "it isn't good my man! At the rate you're going, you will need to close that thing during the next fiscal year at best."

"What about the new business coming in?" I asked.

Silence. I could hear him punching that ten-key calculator with tape reeling. He finally gave me what the increased margin would be on the new business but added, "unless you can get a whole lot more efficient than you are today, that won't be enough to keep you afloat." There was that word again . . . efficient.

I liked Roger. I respected him. He was like me in that he still wanted to play sports. It seemed he was always competing in something or playing in some type of league–bowling, golf, softball. Even though he is several years my elder, to this day I have never beaten him at anything. It seems guys like him that compete, take that spirit to their profession as well. They like to win. They practice winning and expect to win. I knew if I was to win, I needed his help.

I looked at the past year's financial statements and operating metrics. Not good. I looked at any obvious areas for improvement. There were so many, it was scary. Labor and salaries were more than the sales could support. Overtime for both hourly and salary workers was huge, yet we were shipping past due and paying premium freight to supply our customers. It seemed like every metric we had looked bad, yet everyone was working long and hard. What more could I ask?

I decided to take my case to all the hourly people. I wanted to get their thoughts on our operating performance. I'd ask for suggestions and see if they had ideas on how to improve. To do this, I stood at the employee exit doors at the end of each shift for several days. As they would leave, I would ask the ones that would stop and were open to talking if they had a good day. I would get responses such as, "I worked hard. I ran my rate. I did everything that I was asked. I think I did." And so, the story would go. After doing this for all three shifts (we ran production around the clock), I discovered three things: One, they were working hard. Two, most did not really know what was expected of them. Three, they had no real-time feedback on their performance.

I compiled my findings over the next few days and reviewed them with my management team at our next staff meeting. When I gave them the three things, they responded in denial (much as I did when this started). "They must know what kind of job they are doing," the managers said. "We give them feedback all the time on how they are doing. And we sure as heck know the expectations." But did the associates? We went around the room and I asked for specifics on how they would know this. At first some of the managers tried to justify their answers, but their voices would trail off in the end and they'd resign themselves that maybe they didn't know. Maybe our expectations weren't so clear and maybe the performance feedback was lacking.

As we discussed, we also recognized we had similar issues among our management team. We were working hard but not smart. Our measure of doing a good job was if we were tired at the end of the day or if we were working a lot of overtime. If we were doing all of that, we must be doing a good job, right?

Our team was getting way past tired and frustrated. It was one of those feelings of "if it is going to be bad, let's just get it over with." We obviously weren't finding joy in our results or even in the pursuit alone. Our managers were pouring their hearts into this and so were our hourly workers. Surely more work and working harder was not the answer. Like my training runs, I was in search of better methods. I was in search of efficiency.

We discussed ideas as a staff for several weeks. We routinely filled out multiple flip charts of ideas along with pros and cons. Most ideas we came up with were addressing symptoms and not root causes. We were frustrated. We decided to take it back to the production workers and ask them. What else can we do to be more efficient?

We had plant-wide meetings at the beginning of each month after the earnings statement was published. I decided that I would take the opportunity, after getting better but still dismal results, to launch a thirty-day efficiency review. We asked our self-directed teams to meet at the end of each of their shifts to review their performance based on perfection. In other words, if a cell ideally could run 1,000 units in an eight-hour shift, list the actual results beside the 1,000-unit bogie. If it was less or more than the 1,000, write down what happened. We would collect these and have a meeting with each workgroup to review at the end of the month.

Efficiency was more than product output, it included other direct and indirect costs. We made air conditioning components that were high volume but with tight profit margins. If we had to scrap a part, it not only was a loss of material but also all the labor and time needed to produce a replacement part. Excessive scrap could also create overtime or even a missed shipment and extra freight costs. The same was true of unplanned absences; and we, of course, didn't want the drive for efficiency to result in injury. We cared about our workers' well-being, and we needed everyone on deck to plan and execute a successful workday. Having unplanned absences impacted both output and cost. We needed to minimize both. So we also had the teams review and report on scrap, rework, safety incidents, and team attendance.

Tom and Russell were the co-champions of this initiative and compiled the results. Their job was then to meet with each team and establish an improvement goal based on the prior month's performance. We promised, as management, to work on the items they listed as issues to help them reach their target percentage improvement.

We made simple daily scorecards and put them on the line each day for them to collect their results and improvement ideas. We gave each of the items a numerical value to make it quantify more easily for discussion. For example, for every part short or over plan we would say it was -/+ $10 per part. The same for scrap and rework. For unplanned absence, we gave a value of -$100/day while safety incidences were given a value of -$500/incidence. Everything was based around Safety, Quality, Cost, and Delivery. On the flip side, these dollars could be positive if we could run over rate, have a safe month, and zero unplanned absences.

We knew we had less than a year to prove we could be profitable, so time was of the essence. The plan was that Tom, Russell, and I would meet with each team and their supervisor after the thirty-day efficiency review to discuss the performance and talk about what improvements we could make in the next thirty days. After the review, we asked the team to set a percentage improvement goal and track for another thirty days. We'd then repeat the process all over again. We planned for quarterly and annual rewards to give out to each team for goal achievement and the most improved. We decided to call our program "Opportunity Lost."

As timing would have it, I was called out of town to visit customers right before the meetings were to happen. It was critical that we did these on time so I gave strict instructions to both Tom and Russell to make sure we *guided* the team on setting their goals. My fear was twofold. Some teams might set their goals too high, get frustrated, and do nothing; other teams might set a low goal so they could say they achieved it. I specifically told both Tom and Russell to shoot for 15% to 20% improvements. If we achieved that much (which I didn't believe we could), we would be well on our way to making the plant profitable before the deadline to fix it or "whack it."

Tom is the humblest man I know and wouldn't say poo if he had a mouth full of it. When Tom gets nervous or he's trying to make a point he repeatedly says, "right there." So, when I called Tom to see how the goal setting went, he immediately broke out into, "Mark, right there, right there. We met with all the teams and right there they set some pretty high goals."

My blood pressure was rising. This was exactly what I'd said I didn't want. "How much?" I asked more than once, until Tom finally gave a straight reply.

"Mark, right there, right there, they pretty much all said they could eliminate all the waste . . . one hundred percent." To keep from completely boiling over, I decided in my mind that Tom really didn't know what he was saying and that he probably didn't know how to figure percentages.

I called Russell and he immediately went into his salesmanship role which told me that it did not go as I had directed. He basically said the same thing as Tom minus the "right there's" and went on to say that the associates were convinced they could eliminate all missed opportunities. I gave Russell a few choice words about what I thought about their ability to carry out an assignment and said we would talk when I got back into the plant.

A few days later, I called Tom and Russell into my office for further explanation and admonishment. They had the flip charts with them and painfully went through each team and what they thought they could accomplish by next quarter's end. I was still fuming and let them have it. I basically said I would go back to the teams and see what was possible and adjust to fit the real goals.

Once I dismissed them from our meeting, I headed out to the production floor and purposely sought out some of my more challenging teams to start discussing their goals. They all proudly stated their goal of 100% and why they thought they could achieve it. It was hard to argue with them, but in my heart,

I knew there was no way they could meet the goals they were setting. So I told them not to worry if they missed it too badly, we could always adjust the next quarter.

The first month went by and boom, we saw some big improvements. Still nowhere near 100% but way higher than I predicted. After the first quarter, the teams in total achieved over 140% of their goal. I was stunned. My plant accountant was already buzzing that we are about to make some serious cash here. I felt so stupid but so proud. Thank God I was out of town and did not get in the way. Too bad that Tom and Russell had to hear my rantings for almost ninety days. But thankfully, they are strong men and leaders who are willing to stand up to a sometimes-unbearable boss.

I thought back on what we learned from the early days when I was interviewing people as they left the plant. First, we were no longer working hard, we were having fun. We had capitalized on our self-directed work teams to produce un-precedented efficiency thus reducing costs and making the plant profitable. Secondly, we now had clear expectations for everyone. No one had to guess if they were doing a good job and were now being affirmed daily for a job well done. And thirdly, we were measuring our results daily and working toward continuous improvement. We quit furiously reacting to everything wrong. Instead we began tracking results, quantifying our opportunities, and working as a team on solving our problems and creating our next opportunity.

We moved our performance away from the threat of the dreaded "whack" to making serious money on the P&L. Associates were seeing the results of their efforts in quarterly profit-sharing checks. But most of all, we were looked at as a viable operating entity and self-esteem was restored within our team.

I've carried that experience with me for the remainder of my career and have used it time and time again both personally and professionally. Anytime I see a person working excessively hard or who is extremely busy, I think, maybe that person should be lazier. Of course, I mean lazy in the sense of knowing there must be a better way to get the same results with less effort.

Even though I preach this over and over, I have fallen into it time and time again. Sometimes not of my own doing, but I fall into it nonetheless. It's frustrating. It's frustrating to do and frustrating to watch. We ultimately know when it happens, but like a jet fighter in a nosedive, we can almost never pull out of it and ultimately crash.

As with most faults, it is easier to see them in others than yourself. While going through this efficiency learning, I had two key staff members on my Trumann team who would live this dichotomy in front of me every day. One was my production control manager and the other, my quality manager. Both had great results and were very respected in their fields. The production manager, who seemed to move at a snail's pace, always had his work done at the end of the day with what seemed little to no effort. No matter how much you gave him to do, it seemed he just included it with everything else and got the job done. The quality manager, a hyper young engineer, seemed to always be running through the door at the last minute, hair on fire, with his completed work. He was a flurry of activity and his desk and surroundings looked like a sawmill with shavings and piles of remnants everywhere.

Once before an important visit from a key customer, unbeknownst to me, the quality manager literally spent all night in the plant preparing for the visit and had slept a few hours on the conference room table. When the visit was complete and we had received a favorable review, I called in my team to congratulate them on a job well done. It was then that I found out he had worked all night. What was even worse, the team made sure he got special recognition for it. While I joined in with them in their praise for a job well done, I later counseled him for these repeated actions.

At first, he was in denial. He said he had more to do than the rest of the team. He was hurt that I would bring this up considering the results. I was hurt to have to bring it up. In the kindest way I knew how (which at that point in my career, probably wasn't great), I told him this was unacceptable. First, when you must work that hard to accomplish something, you are always teetering on failure. One small slip-up working that close to the deadline will be fatal. Second, it will eventually burn you out or kill you. I needed fresh and productive team members. Finally, working that busily never lets you expand your sphere of influence or lets you take on new things. You will always be too overwhelmed just doing the same stuff over and over.

I am happy to say the quality manager took this lesson and became a beast of productivity. He was promoted several times and eventually became a Lean leader in the healthcare industry, helping and teaching others how to be productive and make their efforts count.

Activity does not equal productivity. Being busy does not mean a lot is getting accomplished. I routinely tell my staff today, "If I ever tell you to work harder, go have me checked for a brain tumor. I want smarter work, not harder work!"

CHAPTER 7

The Joy of Strategic Planning– The Only Thing Worse Than a Bad Plan Is Sticking to It

"'It does not do to leave a live dragon out of your cal-culations, if you live near him.'" –Gandalf, J.R.R. Tolkien, The Hobbit

My wife Stacie, now known as the trophy wife, was given this name several years ago at a church small group gathering by one of my good friends. We would have a meal or snacks after our gathering that quite honestly became the highlight of our meeting. It was at the conclusion of one of these meetings that Stacie served a dish that was over the top. After all the guys loaded up a huge helping, our friend said, "Oh I get it. She has skills too, she's not just the trophy wife." Since Stacie is quite attractive, I frequently refer to her with this name to watch new friends and business colleagues squirm. Stacie almost immediately chimes in saying that she is the first and *only* wife, to which they give out a relieved nervous chuckle.

The trophy wife gave a talk at a women's conference several years ago after the birth of our second child. She was asked to speak about her faith and resilience in raising our two sons, one of whom has Down syndrome. I didn't get to hear the speech firsthand, but from the tons of feedback I received, she must have hit one out of the park.

I later learned she based her talk on the essay "Welcome to Holland" by Emily Perl Kingsley. The essay was about planning for the birth of a normal child, traveling to Italy like everyone else, but ending up in Holland. It was still beautiful but not what was planned. She said that was or could be disappointing unless you found the beauty and fulfillment in the new location. Joy was in adjusting the mindset, tweaking the strategy, and making new plans.

Like the trip to Holland, some of my best strategic planning has not always yielded the planned results. Sometimes the plans fell flat or the desired results didn't materialize at all. Sometimes the issue was my inability to adapt my plans to changing circumstances. Strategic planning is fundamental to success and joy, but adjusting or adapting is of equal importance.

I was asked by some of my running friends to participate in a biathlon several years ago that consisted of a 5K run and a 20K bike ride. I was a runner and had participated in a lot of local races at that point, but I had never biked competitively. I secretly thought of biking as less of a challenge compared to running. It was something those less talented competed in.

While there are varying speeds/degrees of runners, we all sort of looked the same. We trained similarly and wore similar gear. The biggest advantage from one novice runner to the other is genetics and age. Sure, some train harder but overall, we were a pretty homogenous group. Biking, from my rookie viewpoint, was different. They all had bikes, but bikes were bikes and bikers came in all sizes. They were short, tall, heavy, thin, muscular, skinny, or a mixture. It didn't appear to my naive self that genetics or equipment played a significant role in how well you performed, unless you were Lance Armstrong. You just needed a bike and to be in good shape, and that I was.

I was better than the average runner for my age group in the local circuit, and I figured I could nail this event, grab another t-shirt and age-group medal, and go home. In preparation for the event, I spent my training time running. I thought if I could be in great running shape, I could take the running event and then cruise my way to victory, or a respectable finish, on the bike.

I made a training plan that I felt should yield close to a sub-twenty-minute 5K. I then added some mileage to compensate for my time on the bike. I had heard anecdotally that running a 5K was like completing 15K on a bike, so, my training formula was simple. I needed to be able to complete two 5Ks back to back, and then some, and I would have this thing whipped.

On race day, I loaded up my 10-speed in the back of my old powder blue Ford truck and took off for the race. When I arrived, everyone was prepping their gear. I had never attempted anything like this, so I was looking around trying to learn. In a biathlon, there are two starting points or "stages"; the starting line prep areas for the run and the starting line prep area for the bike. Since both sports require different equipment, each athlete puts the appropriate equipment in advance of the race at each stage. I eventually ran into a couple of guys I knew, and they walked me through the process. They instructed me to put my bike in the bike rack along with my helmet and biking shoes so I could make a quick transition after the 5K. Biking shoes? I told them I didn't have different shoes. They looked a little perplexed but blew it off and told me to stage my bike and get to the start line for the 5K.

I quickly discovered I really couldn't use the bike racks because I had a kickstand . . . and fenders. That should have been a clue to how this race might go, but I surmised that I would be even faster as I positioned my bike to the side rather than in the rack. I wouldn't have to wade through all the people to get my bike and I wouldn't have to change shoes. This was going to be a cinch.

I got everything ready (according to my plan) and headed to the 5K start line. Soon the starting gun fired and we were off. I was doing great, leading my age group, and finishing in a respectable sub-twenty-minute time. Now I'd use my running skills and fitness to shine my way to the finish.

I moved quickly to where the bikes were staged. It was easy to find mine, as I expected. I put on my helmet and was off as fast as I could go. I wanted to push at first and get ahead of the pack, then coast from that point forward. This too seemed to be going as planned until a couple of miles into the race when, suddenly, bikes were passing me like cars. I was stunned. Were these guys really in that much better shape? I immediately shifted into my top gear and tried to gain on them or at least keep up. As good as I had conditioned, I figured if I could just hang with them, then I could outsprint them at the finish.

Even after all my adjustments, this was a losing proposition. I neither had the equipment nor the conditioning to compete. EVERYONE passed me. I was so far behind the last person in front of me, I couldn't even see them. I finished the biathlon in

JOYOUS LEADERSHIP • 77

dead last. Worse than that, the race organizers were waiting on me so they could begin the awards ceremony.

I was both embarrassed and humiliated. I had made a plan, but it was an arrogant plan based solely on my own knowledge. I had not done the proper research or even talked to someone with experience. This was a key learning point in my growth. Planning is good. Strategic planning is better.

In our professional lives, we live and die by our strategic plans. Sometimes we have good ones and sometimes . . . well not so great. The best laid plans can get interrupted by forces that are outside our realm of control—economic disasters, terrorist activity, competitive disruptions, or more recently, pandemics. It is our response to the unplanned events that tends to make or break us.

There are also those leaders who seem to never settle on a plan. They spend so much time trying to create the perfect plan, they miss the opportunity altogether. We can fall into this same trap in our personal lives as well. Some people seem driven by a specific end purpose, setting the trajectory of their life for goal achievement. Others seem aimless and wait on circumstances to either make or break them. And then there are those who simply don't take actions that support their stated goal.

I've seen all the above with varying degrees of success. You probably have, too. The most successful and joyful are the leaders that passionately execute a good plan yet remain sensible and nimble enough to react should times dictate it.

Thankfully, during most of my career, my bosses and peers were quite good at grooming me in strategic planning. If anything, we were plan/execution fanatics. Our guard instead had to be making sure we were on track toward the goal and not rapidly veering off in an unplanned direction.

A recent colleague of mine loves sports and uses a lot of coach and athlete quotes. One of his sayings that I really enjoy is a quote from Coach Bobby Knight's first wife Nancy. The story goes that she was supposedly asked the secret to living with Bobby so long. She responded that when he starts ranting and raving about an issue, she tells him, "Bobby, that horse is dead. Get off of it!" In the book *Bob Knight: The Unauthorized Biography*, he states that Nancy posted signs around the house that read, "THE HORSE IS DEAD, GET OFF OF IT."

Sometimes a rich history of doing something the same way tends to make us keep doing it, even if it stops working. This manager uses that saying with his team regularly to get them to "move on" with the new strategy at hand. If a strategy, approach, or tactic doesn't work–GET OFF OF IT.

In my professional career, it always seemed the more successful joyful times were dominated by leaders who were good at strategic planning. Was it always perfect? Definitely not. But they continually tweaked, communicated, and measured to ensure we were tracking toward our established goals.

One of my senior leaders was obsessed with strategic planning and alignment. Any time you went in his office, the strategy could be found on the top of his desk. Depending on the meeting, he would refer to the strategy and challenge the team, "does this fall within our strategy? Does this get us closer to our goal?" Sometimes it would feel as if he were fanatical about strategy to the point that the detail given was painful. I have grown to appreciate this now, but this wasn't always true.

The planned trip to Italy that eventually ended up in Holland ended beautifully. It only required adjustments and change in perspective. The failed biathlon attempt was a strategic failure. The strategy was so poorly researched and fraught with assumptions that it wasn't recoverable and ended in embarrassing defeat. The real joy comes in the execution of a great (or updated) strategic plan.

CHAPTER 8

The Joy of Personal Value—Always Be Worth More Than You're Paid

"Don't worry about being a star, worry about doing good work, and all that will come to you." –Ice Cube

How many times have you said or heard someone say, "I wish I was paid what I was worth?" I hear this far too often. Not just from employees in places I've worked but in the world in general. It's common water cooler talk among many employees. I'm not always sure they genuinely believe what they are saying or if they feel the need to boast about their worth. Unfortunately, it seems most believe they are underpaid.

If you happen to be one of the underpaid, congratulations. You may be one of the good values your company or organization considers as their assets. If you are one of the individuals who have negotiated your perceived true worth, live it up while you can. Life is short.

I learned early in life about being worth more than you're paid. My dad ran his own business most of my formative years and I saw him wrestle firsthand with employees, balancing their vocational worth to the profitability of his business.

He carried this thinking into his role as chief of police. He would say he had some patrolmen who were nothing more than taxi drivers while he had others that were making our little town of Paragould, Arkansas a safer place to live. All the employees were "meeting" the minimal requirements for employment while some were exceeding the requirements of their employment. In other words, they were worth more than they were paid—a good value to the community.

During my dad's career, on two different occasions he ran a service station. The first one was before I was born and the next one was while I was old enough to hang around and help. Service stations in the early '70s were very different from gas stations today. In addition to pumping your gas while you remained in your car, they would check the tire pressure and under-the-hood fluid levels. Also standard was a good cleaning of the windshield, removing all bugs and grime. All this was done for the price of a tank of gas.

The one I was familiar with was located at 104 E. Kingshighway. Today there is a railroad overpass there that obscures the location, but back in the early '70s this was a hotbed location, especially for truckers. While we did our fair share of mechanical work for cars, the real business was diesel trucks.

Emerson Electric had a fleet of trucks a few miles away on Pekin Road. They frequently ran trucks to and from St. Louis that required fuel and maintenance. In addition to these, were several independent and small haulers located on the east side of town. We had dump truck owner operators and several large farms that hauled their own grain.

The one thing that all our customers had in common was a focus on value for their dollar. Families depended on us to keep their vehicles running reliably at a fair price. If we couldn't do it, there were plenty of other places to take their business. The truckers, on the other hand, needed a fair value for them to make money. If it cost too much to maintain their equipment, they either didn't make money or they couldn't be competitive on bidding for a haul.

For my dad to provide this value, he had to assemble a team that was both affordable and capable. I remember several men quickly going through his employment for one reason or the other. It was only the true "valued" employee that he tried to hold on to and even increase their pay as possible. Others either never attained their needed value or once they attained it, demanded a wage so high, the value was no longer there.

We all make decisions like that with our money every day. We not only make this choice with our mechanic but with our plumber, electrician, grocery store, clothing and shoe stores. But we seem to forget that the same value proposition with our employer exists as well. Everyone is looking for the best value for his or her dollar.

When men would come to my dad looking for a job, rarely were they not capable of doing mechanic work. In fact, most of them were quite capable. But capable at what price? What speed? What work ethic? What moral ethic? All those characteristics make up the *value* of the person being hired. Equally important as hiring was retaining that value year after year.

When hired, we obviously were a fair value to our employer. What happens next is almost entirely up to us. This is exactly the position I found myself in several times throughout my career. Some on the positive side, an asset, and some on the negative side, a liability.

My first professional job after college was an excellent lesson in value. I had been hired through a local recruiting agency to work as a sales coordinator and production planner for a family-owned small industrial electronics business. They were a maker of bug zappers, fans, and air purification systems. It was a good business but a very competitive market that was starting to see a lot of the bigger manufacturers begin to play. I was there for less than six months when suddenly they started going through a layoff to cut costs as a result of some lost contracts. I was worth little to the company as far as experience goes, but I was worth lots as far as what I could do earning such a small salary. While I eventually did get caught in the layoff shuffle, I survived longer than I thought I would on sheer value alone.

It took me several years to realize what happened here. I wasn't sure if I should feel flattered or stupid. Did I negotiate such a small salary that it was cheaper to keep me than lay me off? Or was I really perceived so valuable they were trying to retain me? It was probably some of both, and that's okay. That lesson of value would serve me well throughout my career.

Some years later, I was on the other side of the equation. I had been working as a front-line supervisor for Big Red, the plant manager. I would also take on any other special project that he could use me for. I loved being a supervisor, but what I really wanted was a shot at staff management. I had an undergraduate degree in management, and I wanted to "have a say" in how work got planned, scheduled, and completed. Long term my sights were set on being a plant manager, but for now I wanted to either be the production manager or pricing/estimating manager, positions that would allow me to hone my business skills. Those were two jobs currently held by a couple of my peers that I could see myself doing should they ever get promoted or leave the company. I had the education and was fast gaining experience that would equip me to qualify for their roles.

During this time, the automotive companies were under intense pressure to improve quality. The J.D. Power awards were just beginning to rate car companies against one another, and the U.S. manufacturers were rated among the bottom in most categories. This poor rating along with the popularity of Japanese imports was eating into their market share and creating price pressures. Their main response was to improve their supply base, and we were an exclusive supplier to the automotive industry.

About a year after I started, we received our annual quality audit in which we were put on probationary status. We had been given ninety days to clean up our documentation and show a marked effort on continuous improvement, or they would start de-sourcing us to our competitors. As a result of this, I received a small promotion to the quality department as Quality Coordinator. In this role, I oversaw not only implementing quality improvements on critical processes but also cleaning up and controlling the documentation on said processes.

Less than two years after my start date, the pricing/estimating manager position came open when the current manager was promoted to another position at a sister plant. This was good and bad for me all at the same time. The position was available, but it was too soon. I didn't have the tenure or experience to secure this position. And I had competition—the quality manager asked to make a lateral move and get out of his brutal position.

The quality manager in a plant that supplies the automotive industry is considered high stress. Automotive companies demand they received zero defects. In the rare case they do receive a defect, it is to never be repeated. They demand documentation of what is termed "irreversible corrective action." It is up to the quality manager and his staff to make sure this requirement is met. In doing so, their actions can cause friction within the plant and executive management. Sometimes the corrective actions drive up cost and disrupt the current flow of production. It seems they are always in a balancing act between satisfying plant management and the customer.

The quality manager got the position I hoped for, but I was "asked" if I wanted to apply for his now vacant job. I had witnessed firsthand how difficult and stressful the job could be when the audits took place and really wanted no part of them. Big Red called me into his office and affirmed me for the work I had been doing, but quickly agreed with me that this job may be too much too quick. He assured me other opportunities would come and to be patient. Besides feeling totally inadequate to do the job, I didn't see how any job could pay well enough to take the daily beatings from both the customers and the plant. It was a no-win opportunity. The rumor around the plant was the position was so difficult that they were going to recruit from the outside.

I was looking forward to my new boss coming in and taking charge. However, this was not meant to be. While the search was ongoing, I was scheduled to take a day off for an appointment with an allergy specialist. I was recently married, and Stacie and I were living in our small 900-square-foot apartment on Mueller Street. My plans were to sleep in for a few hours and then make the trek to Little Rock to see the specialist. Instead at about 6:00 AM, there was a knock at the front door. I scrambled for a scarce bathrobe while trying to wake up and figure out who in the heck would be at the front door of newlyweds at this time in the morning.

When I finally made my way to the door and opened it, there stood Big Red. He was the last person I expected this time of day. He did live in the subdivision down the road, but it wasn't exactly like we were buds and hung out on the weekend together. As I looked at him, all I could think of was that I must be in trouble for something. "Hey Jerry," I said. "Is there a problem?" He immediately said he needed to come in and talk.

I invited him in, and he and I took a seat on my homemade couch. He started the conversation by telling me the search for a quality manager had not gone well, and the corporate office was getting anxious for it to be filled immediately or they were going to send one of their own to help. Big Red went on to tell me he was not a fan of "help" from the corporate office and that he wanted me to take the job.

Me. Me? A few weeks earlier both he and I agreed this was not the job for me. What had changed? Circumstances. Lack of a desirable outside candidate, a need for some insider experience, quality audit requirements, and corporate pressure. While I didn't understand it then, my value had been increasing over the past couple of weeks and I was totally unaware of it. It's not that I had personally increased my worth by becoming smarter or more experienced, it was the fact that they overestimated their ability to attract an available outside candidate. The benefit of having me in this job was far greater than all perceived cost. I was now the defacto candidate of choice.

My first reaction to this offer was that they wanted me to do the job but do it for nothing. I had already seen the pressure the other guy went through and knew there was no way they would or could compensate me for this amount of stress. The more I declined the offer, the more Big Red was willing to pay. I wasn't looking for more money. I wanted the opportunity to be successful and not have it kill me at the same time. Big Red and I finally came to an agreement that worked for both of us.

While this was a great lesson, I'm not sure I totally understood how good it was until I was running my own P&L (profit and loss) statement. It wasn't until then that I really counted the cost versus the benefit of not only myself but of all my staff. This was especially true when I was the plant manager at Trumann and trying to turn it from a loss to a profit. During that time, I was evaluating every expense versus worth. We were so tight on profit margin that every product, process, and employee had to be worth more than the cost or we were dead.

To reverse the loss equation, I opted for youth over skill. I could hire young engineers right out of college at a better value than hiring expensive experienced professionals by luring them away from their current jobs. What the young workers lacked in experience, I felt we could give them, and then let them grow with the plant as we grew. A win-win for everyone.

At the first hint of profitability, a couple of my younger and brighter engineers asked to meet with me to "talk about their future." I naively said "sure" and looked forward to our meeting. When the meeting started, they immediately went into a story of their worth versus how little they were paid. They listed all the plant's recent successes and the role they played in making that happen.

It was not a pretty sight. They looked both childish and arrogant. It was all I could do to not throw them out right there and say good luck taking your eighteen months' worth of experience and making more somewhere else. Sure, they had done a good job. They had helped the plant get on the road to success. But they had not done it alone. It was with the help of mature skillful mentors that they achieved their success. It was their energy and someone else's wisdom.

I let them keep talking and even encouraged them to keep telling me about their worth. They beamed with misplaced pride and kept going. At one point I asked them, "how much do you think you should make?" This seemed to stump them. I guess they hadn't thought their argument through this far.

Finally, one of them started going through their bills and listed rent, truck payment, food, and a lot of social life expenses. As he went on, his voice seemed to get a little quieter. He seemed less sure of his true "expenses." When he finally ran out of air, I said, "You don't have an income problem, you have an expense problem." I went on to tell them that when I tally up all the expenses they listed, there was no way I could afford them. They would be making more than some of my staff managers.

Their story ended well. They weren't exactly happy but seemed reflective. They both stayed with the plant for several more years and became staff managers later in their careers. One of them thanked me years later for giving him the "expense" problem talk. He said it had served him well as he sought to make his way in the world. This experience taught me as much as it did my two engineers. I remember reflecting on what my true worth to my boss was. What were my true expenses?

I can't even begin to remember the number of times when I took a new job or promotion and had direct reports earning more than I did. My first supervisory role as a welding supervisor, all the welders made more than I did. I even worked longer hours. I remember passing out W-2s at the end of the year and then seeing my own and thinking, *I should have learned to weld.* This continued as I moved up the ranks and supervised salary people. There were always those that earned more than me even though I was their boss. There were a lot of reasons for this. In some cases, they were highly skilled employees in a technical area, like the welders. In other cases, they were more mature and farther along in their careers.

I soon learned to appreciate those scenarios and hoped with each move, this would continue–a subordinate earning more than myself. If I was being entrusted to supervise those that made more than me, then my boss must have believed I was worth it. It meant I had value as an employee.

This really made sense the first time I promoted someone to a position where I knew they weren't going to be the highest paid. I had to figure out how to tell them what to expect. I wanted them to understand as I did that this was a good thing. It meant they were still moving upward while some they supervised might be on a less vertical trajectory.

If this phenomenon is something you can deal with, it will serve you well. If not, you will eventually be paid exactly what you're worth and your career will stagnate. You may disagree but think about it. If you are paid exactly what you are worth, where do you go from there? Can you get another promotion? Can you get another raise? Are you valued by your employer as a "good deal"?

What if the industry or field you work needs to make a cutback? What if they need to reduce their expenses to cut losses or remain profitable? Those that are of better value tend to get a favorable nod, while those with less value get bought out, pushed to early retirement, or simply laid off by job elimination. It doesn't always seem fair but that is reality.

We see this same thing happen in the sports world. The star athlete of a given team demands his worth and finally gets it, only to see the team stagnate–the star athlete falters into good but no longer great. No longer "worth" to the fans what he or she is being paid. While I don't pretend to understand all the sports greats and the dynamics that went into their salaries, I do know some of the greats like Michael Jordan and Peyton Manning didn't take "what they were worth" in order to leave room for some great teammates. This is not only a true test of their humility but also true understanding of the business side of the equation. It left them with a great team and a good run of playoffs and championships, thus making the business worth even more. It also puts less pressure on themselves to continue to prove their worth, allowing them to perform at their best and to be considered a great value by the team and their peers.

In summary, being a good value . . .

1. Keeps you in good standing with your employer
2. Allows you to grow and leaves room for mistakes
3. Is good for team morale
4. Shows a sign of maturity and commitment to the organization

Many believe money can buy happiness, so they strive to get every dollar they can negotiate from their employer. Real joy comes in knowing that you are providing value beyond your pay. If for no other reason, do it for yourself. Work joyfully knowing that your contribution is a good value.

CHAPTER 9

The Joy of Humility– Never Be More Important Than Your Job

"There is nothing noble in being superior to your fellow man; true nobility is being superior to your former self."
–Ernest Hemingway

Very similar to always being worth more than you're paid is the need to never be more important than your job. We've all witnessed this or even been the recipient of someone's self-perceived importance. This arrogance can happen at any level or any income. It does not appear to be a respecter of position or financial net worth. We've all seen the overzealous parking attendant or the doctor at a specialty clinic. Both made it a point to let you know that they were super important and in order for you to get what you needed, you needed to show some form of subservient behavior.

Of course, what I'm really referring to here is humility. To be honest, it is a trait that I never sought or felt like I needed till a few years into my career. I don't know that I was arrogant, but the absence of a desire for humility can certainly express itself in arrogance.

During my formative years as a manager, it seemed the world was teaching us to focus inwardly on confidence. There were a plethora of positive thinking and self-help gurus that were vying for my interest to help me succeed. The problem with most of their messages was the focus was on me. In building this super confidence to succeed, it bred a lot of arrogant and self-centered leaders. Because of my upbringing, I recognized the charlatans early and steered my development away from that group. I was all about bettering myself and trying to be successful, but that group even made me a little queasy.

In my over thirty years in leadership, I have witnessed some of the most humble leaders as well as some of the least. For the sake of learning, I will offer a few of the best and a couple of the worst and what I learned from each. To end the chapter on a positive note, let's start with the less desirable first.

One of my first experiences with someone who thought they were more important than their job was not a leader, but a technician who had "approval" authority. This approval authority was given to him, according to what I was told, not because he earned it, but to get him to buy-in and become a team player. Bad decision. His approval became the signet ring everyone had to kiss before the team could move forward. He wore his approval authority like a badge. He lorded it over everyone and it became a point of contention when trying to move any process forward. It made him feel super important but was a detriment to the organization.

We had a new quality initiative that we had been asked to implement and embrace. I got my team together along with the support groups and outlined what we had been asked to do. As with many corporate initiatives, it was given as a directive but the details of how we got it done was up to the individual teams. We were asked to embrace the mindset of zero defects. We received a two-day training session on the background of zero defects and the shift in thinking that was required to achieve this level of quality. We obviously weren't asked to immediately produce zero defects on our return to work but instead to take on the endless pursuit of improvement until all defects were eradicated.

As production supervisors, we were to review our individual departments and look for areas that produced defects. Making air conditioner plumbing wasn't expensive but every dollar counts. Plus, the fewer defects an area made, the less likely a customer was to receive a defective part. While individually our impact might seem small, collectively we could make a significant improvement in our product and customer satisfaction.

However, when we returned to our jobs, the technician took it upon himself to not approve anything unless there were zero defects. The result was that he single-handedly shut down a department and eventually most of production. His peers tried to reason with him. His supervisor tried to reason with him. They wanted to believe he just didn't understand the concept of steady improvement to reach zero defects. They were hoping to make him understand it was a pursuit, a mindset.

This went on for the better part of the morning and it was starting to get expensive to have this many people idle, not to mention the lost production and potential missed shipments to our customers. If at any point he sensed that his decision might get overridden, he would spout off, "then you must not support zero defects." There was almost no way the manager could win.

The above situation is all too common, and we've all seen it. It may be a little different in your experience, but we all know that one person. It's almost as if every organization must have one. Even if that person leaves, another one surfaces to take their place.

In this case, the manager was forced to reassign the technician to a lesser level of authority. Even though he received a lot of training and career counseling after the failed assignment, he had limited his growth. Your level of humility almost always determines your level of success . . . especially sustained success.

The second example is more of a type than a specific person that I call Mr. Cool, though it can be a man or a woman. Mr. Cool is an executive who, in his mind, "has finally arrived" and he demands that everyone knows it. He still possesses some good leadership traits, but his arrogance now eclipses and degrades his effectiveness. Mr. Cool changes from the person that earned the promotion to some mythical executive, a being he has conjured up in his mind. He goes from being a competent leader at his previous level to worrying about his job title, office size, and how people should address him. It would be Dilbert-like comical if it weren't playing out as reality in front of everyone's eyes.

You can insert your own name for Mr. Cool. We've all known him. I've known several in my years in leadership and it never gets easier to stomach them. My most memorable was a guy that had done well in his career to a point. He got a promotion and came in the next day a different person. He was dressed completely differently, a little over the top. He decked out his office with new decor. Eventually, he started driving a newer car. Worst of all, he was very condescending to those who were once his peers. It was painful to watch this guy self-destruct. He became the talk of the office. Most of us hoped it was a phase and he would eventually get comfortable in his newfound role and humble himself back into the leadership and work ethic that was once so valued.

In his case, however, it only got worse. There were minions that found him and played to his ego. They knew if they could stroke him, he would throw favors their way. He would feed them so he could receive even more platitudes from his worshipers. It was sickening and short-lived. His manager tried to reason with him and show him the error of his ways. He was sent to a leadership class and came back emboldened. Not the desired result at all. Within a few short months, he was escorted out the door, his disbelief that the company hadn't recognized his greatness evident.

I'm sure there were warning signs early in his career that should have been addressed. As my mom would say, "he got too big for his britches." I used to not really understand exactly what that meant, but I knew vanity and pride was at the heart of it. And now I get it. The world has many of them.

The best attribute anyone can have to prevent self-importance from clouding his or her judgement is servant leadership. Bishop Dale C. Bronner puts it this way: "If serving is below you, leadership is beyond you." Put that into practice if you haven't done so already. Look for that trait in people that you may want to promote to a leadership position one day. Look at the best leaders that are adored by others and you won't have to look too far to see this trait in their lives.

I've been blessed in my career and personal life to have witnessed some of the best when it comes to humble leadership. My friend Greg is one such leader. I met Greg while being asked to serve on a nonprofit board that serviced adults with special needs. The nonprofit advocated for the handicapped and worked to improve their quality of life by providing housing, jobs, and better healthcare. Greg was the CEO of this nonprofit and looked the part. He was always dressed in a suit and tie when I saw him, salt/pepper hair perfectly groomed, with a command for the room when he spoke.

I must admit that when I first met him, I was skeptical. I thought this was too good to be true, and he probably got appointed to this position by having the right political connections and was benefiting from other people's misfortunes. Not that he was a bad guy. He wasn't. But we've all seen this type of position being held by "good" people who want the notoriety and perks, both monetary and political.

However, after serving with Greg a few months, my preconceived notions began to fade. I saw him talk passionately about the plight of these adults and their need for legitimacy as humans. He would sometimes become angry and tear up if certain legislation or circumstance minimized our residents. He would "get in the face" of anyone who didn't respect or recognize our residents. It was sort of cool.

My office wasn't far from his office and he would occasionally ask me to lunch. I loved this and insisted on paying so I could learn more about the work he was so passionate about. On one such lunch date, he was talking about the men in our care and was tearfully describing how they don't get to enjoy some of the things that "normal" adults get to enjoy. They rarely get to go to St. Louis to see the Cardinals play. They never got to see wrestling. They never grill out with the family and just hang out. "We must change that," he said. He had the ability to make me want to stop eating immediately and load up the bus for a ballgame. He always had a plan. But more than a plan, he had inspiration.

A few weeks after that lunch talk, we had our monthly board meeting. There was Greg at the head of the table all dressed up and dapper as usual. But this time his grin was more boyish than usual. Did I mention that Greg is retired? Sort of. At least, he's old enough to have retired after working in other similar jobs as an advocate for the handicapped and a long stint with the state government. Most men of his stature would be a cliché. Living their best life to the fullest as the world defines it. But not Greg. He's really living.

Greg couldn't wait for the meeting to start to tell everyone what a great idea that he and one of the other board members pulled off for the men in our care. They decided to give the care-takers a night off and have the guys gather at the campus for a cookout and Pay-Per-View wrestling. He could hardly tell the story for all the joy and laughter in his voice. He finished up by saying all this cost less than $100, which we found out later he had paid out of his own pocket.

He went on to share a few photos of the evening and all the festivities. The men were laughing and enjoying themselves like every other red-blooded American that gets to participate in such craziness. He had given them a gift. He had given us a gift. And from the look on his face, he had received the best gift of all.

Greg does own a pair of jeans and a sweatshirt. He can look like a regular guy. Even his perfectly groomed hair can have a wisp of carefree in it. Greg doesn't just sit behind his CEO desk delegating and giving orders. He can often be found sitting with the residents talking, serving, and joking. Joyous leadership wasn't just being taught; it was being modeled for all of us.

So, which leader do you want to be? Which leader do you want to serve? I think the answer is obvious but not always evident in our pursuit. We sometimes forget in the middle of the competition and heat of the battle.

Humble leaders serve. Humble leaders don't care who gets the credit for a job well done. Humble leaders turn the pyramid of authority upside down. Greg modeled this when he gave up his own weekend to become the caretaker for the evening or the bus chaperone for the ballgame. These are the jobs that most people don't want to do. These aren't the jobs that get featured in those local magazines for and about the social elite's philanthropic efforts through fundraising balls and galas. A lot of people can write checks (and thankfully do), but few people spend their free time with those of a less or social status.

Let's be a Greg. Let's be joyous and humble leaders.

CHAPTER 10

The Joy of Resiliency– Training Is Required

"The human capacity for burden is like bamboo–far more flexible than you'd ever believe at first glance."
–Jodi Picoult, *My Sister's Keeper*

Have you had one of those days, weeks, months, or a time in your life when you felt you can't endure one more burden? It's a time we all go through when it seems like one bad thing or one tough challenge after another keeps coming at us with no relief in sight. We sometimes describe it to others as a "breaking point." It could be health issues, financial issues, family issues, or just a lot of personal stuff piling up. My intent is not to minimize a time like this, but to point out that in the majority of these times, we don't break. Instead, we endure and become even stronger as a result of our trials. There is joy to be found in that hard-won strength.

Of course, if we do become broken, we must seek professional help. There should never be any shame in that. Even the act of reaching out and receiving help is a step towards building resiliency. So never be embarrassed if that is part of your resiliency story. I would even argue it should be the cornerstone.

It would be nice if building resilience to some of life's challenges worked the same way as how we build immunity to a disease like smallpox or polio. Get a vaccination and voilà, we are immune. Unfortunately, personal resilience doesn't work that way.

As I've mentioned, earlier in my adult life I ran marathons. That meant a lot of training. I needed to get in shape to build a resilience to the toll all the miles would have on my body. When people ask me about marathons and if they are hard, I say, "Yes." But the hardest part is all the training. There are a lot of miles on the road with yourself. As one of my friends used to say, you really must like yourself to spend that much time together.

Because of my experience with this popular endurance sport, I've been asked to coach a few people on their first marathon. When first asked, I wasn't sure I liked the idea of going from a participant to a coach. But once I began, I found I enjoyed helping someone achieve their goal and I learned a little more about myself.

The first few people I trained were standard runners. They were already active and fit but had never completed an extreme event such as a marathon. The prescription was simple. Based on goals and how many miles they were already logging each week, we would make out a daily running/training plan. We would build on the plan by adding a few miles or speed training each week that would crescendo about a week before the event. This was all pretty standard stuff. Other than a little coaxing and talking about physiological changes they may experience; it usually went according to plan. It became apparent rather quickly for the student that there was no cheating or shortcut to successfully completing 26.2 miles.

The most difficult part to teach was a part of the race called the wall. It occurs somewhere around the twenty-mile mark when a runner's glycogen or stored energy within the muscles is depleted. While it is biological in nature, it plays on the emotions. The runner can become defeated, combative, extremely sad, or even depressed. The wall is where the marathon loses most of its participants. Even though I would tell every student about this phenomenon, most would give me, at best, a perplexed look or stare in disbelief. It was as difficult as describing a sunrise to a blind man. There were limited words or comparisons to use.

My first experience with the wall was at my first marathon. I had been warned about it from other veteran marathoners, but it really didn't resonate till I faced it in person. I had convinced myself that I could minimize it or avoid it altogether by training hard and being mentally tough. I had read about it, and it *was* avoidable for many of the elite runners. But even they had races where it hit them unpredictably and for no known reason.

Like many novice marathoners, I hit the wall around the twenty-mile mark. At this point in the race, the runners are thinning out and you already have a feeling you are running alone. I only had a 10K (6.2 miles) left to go. I had completed a ton of 10Ks. My confidence should have been high. But my hip muscles had started to tighten, and my gait was fumbling. When I saw the hill off Riverside Drive in Memphis, I let out a few choice words in my mind to the race organizers for mapping out such a stupid course and placing a hill in an obviously stupid location. It was a small hill that should have been minimal effort, but my rational mind had checked out. I was alone and there was no one to emotionally pick me up. It was cold and raining. I had blisters on my feet and chaffing on my thighs. My nipples had started to bleed from the chaffing of my jersey. I was a mess and was wondering why I would even sign up for such a stupid event. The 6.2 miles left until celebration seemed insurmountable at this point.

As I started to climb the hill, I hurt. I let out a quiet cry and tears started running down my cold but sweaty face. I slowed for a few seconds and even walked. I don't know if it was audible or not, but I said, "screw it." It was then I started remembering the veteran marathoner's advice. "Just put one foot in front of the other—no matter how slow, just don't stop. Get inside your head and you control the thinking, not your body. Focus with the end goal in mind and how it's going to feel when you have kicked its ass to the curb." The list of potential encouraging statements went through my head like stock ticker prices on Wall Street.

After what seemed like an eternity, I reached the top of the hill and was running on flat ground once again. My hips had loosened a little and the cloud of dread, depression, and fatigue were lessening. I knew I had beaten the wall. Tears were starting to flow again, but this time tears of joy. Sure, I had another hour of running enjoyment, but I now knew how to press through. I owned that wall.

While I learned a lot about physical and emotional resilience that day, I learned even more during my last coaching session. Brooks was a little different than all my previous students. She was the young widow of my best friend Phillip who had died of pancreatic cancer a couple years prior. She wasn't a runner, and we would be starting from scratch. While I wanted to help, I was not hopeful that this would end successfully. I lived in a different state so being able to watch her stride, gait, and any pronation would be impossible. I would have to rely solely on her describing any issues or concerns. When I asked her for a goal, instead of the typical race time or fitness goal, it was an emotional response to everything she had been through. She had several small reasons, but paramount for her was this: she wanted to prove to herself and her children that she was a tough and capable mother.

I remember thinking, *my gosh, isn't what you've been through enough proof? You've experienced the tragic death of your husband, raising two young children, working, and filling the role of both mom and dad. That's badass in my book. What other proof do you need?*

We exchanged several emails, calls, and texts over the next few days prior to the start of the training. This was mostly me trying to convince myself that this was something we could do. I knew it was going to be hard, but I was caught up in it emotionally as well. It was personal. Good or bad, this was going to impact her for years to come. I couldn't let my best friend's widow fail.

As with all my students, we talked about training wear, shoes, socks, nutrition, and hydration. She had done her homework on most of this and was clarifying things she had read or heard. We then began with the daily training plan and how we would add miles each week to get her closer to the 26.2-mile goal. We even discussed finding running groups or maybe an occasional training partner to help ease the loneliness on the road, particularly during some of the longer runs.

The training was going well. I would text several times during the week and email occasional articles that I thought relevant. She intermittently ran with a friend who had signed up for the same marathon to break up the training regimen. I was moderately hopeful until she called one day about a stress injury. She said she was going to take the week off and had an appointment with an orthopedic specialist early the next week. She was frustrated to the point of tears. I lied, assuring her we would overcome, that it was a temporary setback, even though I wasn't sure myself.

After a steroid injection, a week off, and some modifications to the training program she was back on track. We were both nervous about the injury, but all seemed to be holding together.

The training program called for one long run of twenty miles. She asked me, "so, just because I can complete twenty miles, what makes you so sure I can do 6.2 more."

I had been dreading this question, but for now, I said, "think of it as being almost done with only a 10K (6.2 miles) to go. Since you've done a 10K before, you already know you can do it."

I was reserving talking about "the wall" for later. I thought we might not even get that far in the training and the whole wall conversation wouldn't be necessary. Also, with everything else she had been through in the past few years, I really wasn't sure what words to use. She would understand the feeling, but was she ready to face an emotion like that again?

However, soon training was basically complete, and it was time for "the wall" talk. She had already heard something about it from her training friend and other runners, so it wasn't a total surprise. I spent very little time describing it—she got it. Instead, I spent my time on how to navigate through it.

Our plan was this. I asked her to focus her emotions on something that she really cared about. It had to be something she would fight or even die for if necessary. I also asked her, if possible, to carry a reminder of it with her. Put it in a pocket, wear it, or hold it in her hand and when the wall seemed the biggest, touch it, look at it, and squeeze it. If you can do that for a couple of miles until the emotions and fatigue are in check, you can make it to the end.

Race day finally arrived, and Stacie and I were there to cheer her on. We had pre-mapped our route so we could walk and see her at several locations on the run. I made a point to make sure we would see her at the wall. If need be, we were going to walk/run alongside for emotional support to make sure this run was a success.

We saw Brooks at the start of the race and again at several other points along the route before we walked over to the mile 19-20 interchange and waited. I was nervous, excited, and almost sick to my stomach. I was having doubts but hopeful. As we waited, we saw people running, walking, or quitting in disgust.

Finally, we thought we saw a familiar gait, clothes, and hat. And there she was, still running! We jumped out from around the barrier and started running beside her. She had tears, either from joy or the cold, but she was happy and determined. As we ran beside her she confidently said, "I'm going to make it." She assured us she was fine and would see us at the finish line. She had beaten the wall.

We had a quick celebration with her at the finish line and then left her with her friends and family. It was a mission accomplished and Brooks had a new determined look that she didn't possess a few hours earlier. She had achieved both physical and mental resilience. It wasn't a guarantee that all issues were going to be smooth sailing from here on out, but she had mastered the process. She had developed a tool. That was guarantee enough.

I wondered what she had in her possession to get her through the wall, but never asked. I figured it was none of my business. But a few days after the race, I received an emotional text with photos of what she carried with her throughout the race. It was a locket that Phillip bought for her early in their relationship while on a mission trip. She also carried a key with her with the inscription "Hope" engraved on it. It was a gift that she and Phillip received when he was battling cancer.

Later in the week, I received a Thank-You card in the mail with the "Hope" key enclosed. She told me to keep it. It had served her well and felt it was time to pass it on. She also sent me a Yeti tumbler with "The Greatest Coach" printed on the outside. We had won.

Brooks had found a way to develop resilience. She discovered that a locket and key, properly focused, could transcend a difficult circumstance. Not just physically, but emotionally as well. I had given her a tip, but she developed a tool that, practiced regularly, would benefit her for the rest of her life.

As leaders, we will face the need to be resilient. Maybe not the wall type resilience every time, but the need will come. Sometimes it's the little things that chip away at you day by day.

Over time leadership fatigue sets in and you must call on that inner emotional energy–the intestinal fortitude that allows you to approach the hill with confidence knowing that you can overcome. The team will be depending on you to be the veteran runner, the leader that has already faced and successfully overcome other challenges. Your experience will be the team's confidence.

In my career, there have been dark leadership days. Days when unpopular and tough decisions had to be made. Decisions that impacted people's livelihood and careers. Many times, after work at night, I would go home and moan, "Why me? Why am I faced with this challenge?" A little private pity party is okay. It's part of the process of getting up that hill. Just don't stay there. People have trusted you to lead, to make those tough decisions. As long as you've built up some resiliency along the way, you will beat the wall. And what is even sweeter, others will too.

So, how is your resiliency going? More likely than not, you've already been required to draw on that strength. How did you do? No worries if you feel like you could have done better. That's part of the joy. You can try again. The only failure is quitting, skipping over it, or ignoring it altogether. While struggles aren't fun, much like the marathon, training (small struggles) is necessary for us to develop.

If you are a person of faith, there is a verse in the New Testament book of James that describes how we should face struggles.

Dear brothers and sisters, when troubles of any kind come your way, consider it an opportunity for great joy. For you know that when your faith is tested, your endurance has a chance to grow. So let it grow, for when your endurance is fully developed, you will be perfect and complete, needing nothing. [James 1:2-4 (NLT)]

I have heard people say that life is like a marathon. So ask yourself, how are you training? Do you have a coach?

When an unplanned event (stress injury) happens, and it will, what will be your response? What happens when you face "the wall?" Will you give in or develop resilience? What emotion, idea, or dream are you willing to fight or even die for that will transcend any discomfort while you are pursuing your mission? Let's be a Brooks. Let's choose the joy of resiliency.

CHAPTER 11

The Joy of Generosity–
More Than a Tithe

"No one has ever become poor by giving." –Anne Frank

The best way to not be invited back to speak at any gathering is to speak on giving. I'm not sure I really believe that, but the topic does tend to make a few people squirm. There's an old joke about a pastor preaching on sin. As he preached, the parishioners were all nodding their heads in agreement on each sin he chose to denounce. Since everyone was in such agreement, as the pastor was closing his sermon, he veered off on the topic of giving. One old gentleman turned to the other and said, "he went from preaching to meddling!" My aim here is not to meddle, but to add yet another way to add joy to your journey.

My good friend Shannon and I like to discuss things in confidence, and we're not afraid to tackle topics many people avoid. It's always good to have a couple of friends that will still like you even after you reveal your honest inner thoughts and demons. We don't talk that often now that we live in different cities, but when the opportunity arises, we usually end up on some deep philosophical topic or a conversation about religion.

One time we got on the topic of finances and budgeting. He asked me about my philosophy on money. I immediately went to personal finances—not having debt and always putting something back for retirement and a rainy day. As an afterthought, since we are both church-goers, I threw in the part about tithing to God. Shannon, being a true friend, said that was great and that he expected nothing less from a guy like me. I thought my response sounded canned and boring. So I asked his philosophy.

I loved his answer. It went something like this: *"I call it the 70/10/10/10 rule. All of us live on a certain percentage of our income. Some of us live on 100%. That is, everything coming in goes right back out. Some live on 90%, giving, say, 10% to church. Some live on 80%, give 10% to church, and put 10% into savings. Some of us, if we're honest, live on 110-120%—we're using Visa and American Express to fund a lifestyle of living beyond our income. I try to live on 70%, give 10% to church, put 10% in savings (pay yourself first!), and give 10% away. Nothing in your life will give you quite the satisfaction and joy as giving away money."*

As with most of my conversations with Shannon, they usually don't fully sink in till a few days later. The more I thought about what he said, it really started to make sense. There really is nothing like the freedom to be able to give money away to a cause that you support. Being financially bound and having to pass up opportunities to help is soul crushing. Being liberated to give is a joy like none other.

I had always tried to do as he described but never purposefully. Never as part of my overall equation. Since that conversation, Stacie and I have tried to adopt "Shannon's Rule" as I call it now. The results are just as he promised. There really is no other satisfaction and joy like being able to give away money. This joy doesn't come from accolades or recognition. If that's the reward you're looking for, you will get cheated. Use this 10% for what you're passionate about or for that sudden cause that presents itself that needs your help.

Try this with your budget. If you must, start small, but start. What may seem small to you will be hugely empowering and life giving as you get the hang of it. It will give you a whole new set of lenses in which to view life. It indeed will be joyful.

The first person outside of my family to have a major impact of giving on my life was a family friend named Burl. Burl and his wife Francis had been close friends of our family for as long as I could remember. After my dad passed away during my junior year of high school, Burl always seemed to keep a check on me, as good family friends should and do. He would routinely catch me in the lobby at church and ask me how I was doing. I genuinely felt he was interested in my well-being, and he was. He continued to be there for me throughout my college days all the way through graduation.

Burl was a very successful used car dealer and no doubt much of his success was due to his integrity and generosity as a human being. I've seen him forgo a sale because he didn't think he had a car to fit what the shopper needed or was looking for. That says volumes, especially given the reputation of used car dealers.

Once I graduated college, I was in serious need of a car. The car I was driving was a repaired "totaled" car with over 150,000 known miles. The reason I say "known" is because it was very common back in the '70s to buy a car that had the miles "rolled back" to make the car seem newer and allow the seller to ask a higher sales price.

I had finally landed my first career job and gave Burl a call. I told him I needed a car and the monthly payment I could afford. My only collateral was my "totaled" '72 model Oldsmobile Cutlass which would probably be bought for salvage. I knew it wasn't much to work with, but I would take about anything as long as it was reliable and would get me back and forth to work.

He said he would be on the lookout and try to find something that would be dependable as well as something I would like. A few weeks passed when my phone rang at work one morning. It was Burl. He asked if I could get the afternoon off and come take a look at a car he had picked out.

On my way to his shop, the A/C went out on my Cutlass. It was literally falling apart piece by piece daily. When I pulled up, he told me to get all my personal items out of my car and hop in his. He wouldn't take no for an answer. As soon as I gathered up my cassette tapes, he had another man jump in my car and drive it off. I remember watching it leave the lot and asking, "Burl, what are you doing with my car?"

"Sold it," he replied. I was starting to get a sick feeling in the pit of my stomach. What if I didn't like the new car? What if I couldn't afford it?

We started driving toward downtown Paragould with me quizzing him about where we were going and what kind of car he had found. He kept repeating to trust him. After a few minutes, we arrived at Horner Motor Company and Burl pulled up right in front of the Pontiac Firebirds.

"Which one of those would you like?" he asked.

In the firmest voice I could muster, I said, "Look, I can't afford any of these and I hope I can get my car back." But as much as I argued and stuttered, he kept reassuring me to trust him and we would work it out.

I finally gave in and said the navy-blue Firebird. I still remember to this day thinking that was the coolest car ever. The '81 Firebirds looked a lot like Burt Reynolds' Trans Am in *Smokey and the Bandit*. While I didn't want to look like I had copied ol' Burt, I was still a young man and looking for something just as cool.

Burl motioned me to follow him to the sales office. He walked in and told the poor salesman that we needed that car for the small amount I could pay per month and asked what he could do. The salesman half snickered and said that we were a long way away from the right number. Burl told him he didn't quite understand, we needed the payment at that level and he told the guy to work backwards and see what it would take.

When Burl was done negotiating, not only did I get behind the wheel, the car was in my name without a cosigner. Burl wrote the man a check and kept telling me to shut-up and we would worry about the money later. He assured me that it was okay to take my time to pay him back. It was a gentleman's agreement. The real payback, he insisted, was for me to help others someday when I was able.

I was able to pay him back in a few payments over the next two to three years by using a couple of tax refunds and a bonus from work. I still felt like I needed to pay him more. Maybe some interest or something. He again reiterated that all he asked of me was to do the same for someone else someday.

The lesson from Burl has remained with me to this day. Generosity as a rule doesn't happen nearly enough. True paying forward needs to be risky. We easily give to our church, close friends in need, and family. Outside of these boundaries is where the true difference is made.

How many times has something crossed your radar, but you recognized it too late to act on it? Maybe it was a panhandler, a person whose car broke down on the side of the highway, or simply someone struggling with day-to-day life. We often wait for opportunities to present themselves, and then react and give. While that's a good thing, that's passive giving. True joy is found when you are proactive. Here are a few suggestions to make giving back more purposeful:

1. Plan how much is in your discretionary give-away fund.
2. Think of a situation, cause, or charity that makes you passionate. What can you do to help? Money, time, both?
3. Put it in your daily planner or a sticky note on the fridge. Make it visible so you won't forget.
4. Don't just write a check and send it in the mail. Go look at the hurting eye to eye if possible. This needs to be personal.
5. Look for multiple opportunities. It's great to give every month to a specific cause but if you aren't careful, after a while it feels like the church tithe—it becomes mechanical, without a lot of thought. Remember, this giving is for you. It's for your inner peace and renewal. Have fun with it.
6. Pay it forward. This has gotten a lot of attention over the years as almost a game. Take it to the next level if you can by seeking out someone in advance to pay it forward.

Get the family involved and have fun by secretly blessing someone.

Maybe you, like me, have been the recipient of "giving back." Think back on a time when a timely word, meal, or money made all the difference in your day. It may have been a simple gesture, or it may have been something that literally saved your life. As good as it feels to receive, there is nothing like being the one able to give. With the bounty we have on this earth, we could revolutionize the world if, for just one day, everyone that is able would find a way to give back and bless someone else. Oh, what a world it would be. The receiver would have their load lightened and the giver would be blessed in knowing they had contributed to the good of another human being.

As a leader, generosity is necessary. This will define your humanity and will show through in your leadership. You will become more aware of the needs of those in your care. Better humans make better leaders. Your generosity will influence your family, workgroup, and company in which you serve.

Good leaders are not only generous with their finances, but also with their time. They take time to listen, mentor, and show empathy. They use their gift as a leader to champion social causes such as racial injustice, handicapped rights, climate change, and hunger. Leaders will find joy in giving to something bigger than themselves or their job.

If you want to experience joyful leadership, try Shannon's rule. Be a Burl. Give joyfully.

CHAPTER 12

The Joy of Renewal–
A Dry Season

"The dry seasons in life do not last. The spring rains will come again." –Sarah Ban Breathnach

Oxford dictionary defines renewal as an instance of resuming an activity or state after an interruption. We sometimes see renewal used when talking about city urban areas that need revitalized for the safety and curb appeal of the community. In human terms, these are the things we do to revitalize and update ourselves such as our physical appearance, health, or skillset. The "interruption" we experience as individuals may be hard to recognize. It may creep up on us and we stay in a funk and not even realize we are there. Even when we do realize the need for change, it may be less clear what we need to change or how much.

The reason this may be less evident is that things are still working . . . sort of. They at least don't feel broken enough to bother fixing. Life just seems to be a little stale, not as joyous as it once was. You zombie through the day. It could be that you are unaware but the change is noticed by those closest around you–your family, peers, staff, or coworkers may think you're "not yourself" or "off your game." Unless they're really tuned in, they may not notice either.

The good thing is once you recognize the need, renewal tends to be fun and refreshing. Sometimes the prescription is as simple as rest, exercise, refocus, new learning, or renewed friendships and relationships. A little tweak can sometimes refresh the mind and refocus our vision.

I've been blessed and fortunate to change job assignments about every five to seven years. The reason I say blessed is because I become stale after about year six. I didn't start to realize this until an assignment change early in my career. I noticed afterwards I began experiencing some excitement, new learnings, and self-renewal. While I was excited to get a new role, I wasn't expecting the accompanying feelings.

Unfortunately, I spent little time examining those new feelings and was soon drawn into my new assignment and life moved on. Another six years rolled by, and it was around midlife crisis time when I noticed I was getting complacent, maybe even a little bored. I thought, *maybe this is what success and mid-life feels like.* The job was going well, the family was thriving, and Stacie and I seemed to be in a good place in our marriage. Why change?

I didn't have any real red flags, but there were subtle things that I started noticing like less excitement or eagerness to do much of anything. I plodded to work and did my business travel mindlessly. I seemed to be making all the right decisions, just as I had learned and was trained, but with little thought. My staff was performing well but even they seemed bored or uninterested in meetings or while working on projects.

This went on for a good while. Some days, with some real effort, I seemed to do better and would lead better. Other days, like a hidden snare, I was caught back up in the monotony and resumed operating mindlessly.

I needed a change.

When I get caught up in my own mind, I usually visit my favorite counselor—my wife Stacie. She's always the levelheaded one in the family and keeps me from operating from my emotions alone. I told her about my struggles and boredom and how I hated even going to work. I said I wasn't sure I could do this job for another fifteen to twenty years. The mere thought of that almost made me suffocate.

Stacie convinced me that it really wasn't that bad and that I just needed a break. I was facing burnout and her solution was a family vacation. It was spring, and the boys were in school. Stacie, the ultimate trip planner, discovered a time when our oldest son was going to be traveling through Georgia on a choir trip with school. She worked out a deal with the choir director to drop him off after the tour at the Atlanta airport to board a plane for Orlando so we could all spend a long weekend at Disney World.

Of course the boys were excited, but I must admit I was too. This seemed the perfect combination of getting away from work—rest, fun, and visiting one of the most creative places on earth. Stacie loved the idea of much-needed family time and that she didn't have to cook.

I hoped renewal was this simple, that I would return home rested, refreshed, full of energy and creativity. I'd hear people talking about this remedy quite a lot, I had just never felt

I needed it. Of course, in the past, I had taken time off work and had gone on vacations, but never for the defined reason of renewal.

When we had completed day two of this wonderful vacation, I was still getting a case of the Sunday dreads in the evening and it was only Friday. You know the Sunday dreads. It's that feeling you get when instead of enjoying the end of a fun and restful weekend, you start dreading Monday. Your heart rate goes up, anxiety increases, and before you know it, you are so worked up that you can't sleep because you're thinking about work tomorrow. The alarm goes off Monday morning and all that weekend renewal is cancelled out by sleep deprivation and anxiety from Sunday night.

After dinner and returning to our condo, while the kids were holed up staring at their digital devices, Stacie and I jumped into the hot tub for my next counseling session. I told her that while this vacation was fun, I almost suffocated just thinking about going back to work. The renewal wasn't working.

I went into all the things that were mundane and stifling. I was tired of wearing khakis, button down shirts, and golf shirts with company logos. The travel routine of planes, hotels, and meetings had become tedious. I was irritated by overused business vernacular that could be turned into a bingo card: out of the box, paradigm shift, move the needle, low-hanging fruit. You get the idea. I also mentioned things about myself that I didn't like. I had been sporting a short beard since before we were married. I was losing my hair and developing a dad bod. I looked so stereotypical of what I hated; it was nauseating.

Stacie, taking a gamble, suggested I shave my beard. Not that shaving my beard was going to fix this renewal issue, but maybe it would spur me on to something. Not sure what but something. I didn't think this was a good idea because my skin had not seen daylight for almost twenty years. However, her reasoning was sound. We were in Florida and had enough time to tan before we went back. And if I really hated it, I would have time to grow some of it back before anyone knew the difference.

I'm not the king of style and I depend on a lot of people giving me advice on what I should wear and how to keep my personal appearance somewhat up to date. As I age there is only so much available to work with, it is challenging. If you are like me and you can't objectively discern your own style, it might be a good idea to find a trusted person to help you navigate.

We got out of the hot tub, trimmed the beard as short as we could with the trimmers I always travelled with, then shaved the remainder with a razor. I felt naked. Tate cried actual tears and wanted nothing to do with me. Stacie and Jared just looked on trying to decide if this was a good thing or not.

It turned out to be a good thing, but it had nothing to do with my looks, or style for that matter. I was amazed by how many people didn't notice. They might have recognized something was different but brushed it off as new shoes. Susie, my admin, marched me into my boss, The Big Guy, and announced, "Tom, do you see anything different about Mark?" He looked me over and didn't have a clue. She finally told him I had shaved my beard. He just chuckled and said, "Yes, I see that now. You look great." He put his head back down into the *Wall Street Journal* and never brought it up again.

It was drastic enough for me though that it made me reexamine everything. I was living in a paradigm of my own making. I started questioning not just my personal life but my professional life as well. I had relearned the word "why." It was refreshing.

We've all done this, right? We rock along with old paradigms, concepts, and styles because they worked for us, so we unwittingly stick with them. We intuitively know we should challenge ourselves, but it's normal to stay the path of least resistance. Like Newton's first law of motion, "a body at rest will remain at rest unless an outside force acts on it, and a body in motion at a constant velocity will remain in motion in a straight line unless acted upon by an outside force." It usually takes prompting to get us to change or question if we even should change.

There really is joy in renewal, but we must recognize the need. We may need an outside force such as an honest and true friend or mate to help us. Of course, I'm talking less about personal style and more about inner renewal. But just as personal style requires updating over the years, inner renewal is important and needed on a frequent basis.

Since that first personal renewal experience, I have made renewal more purposeful, almost calendar-driven. I plan time to purposely reflect on my performance, influence, leadership effectiveness, and yes, even personal style. For me, this time seems to work best at the beginning of the new calendar year. Please note. This is not lofty New Year's resolutions. I personally don't do New Year's resolutions. It has nothing to do per se with it being a new year. This just happens to be the planning period that works for me. It happens to coincide with my company's fiscal year, so it seems to be a natural fit to evaluate my personal prior year's effectiveness and learnings and encapsulate that into next year's objectives and planning. You can pick your own best time.

When I say "I" reflect, it is not just "I." I seek out feedback from peers, subordinates, and family. I look for quantitative data as well. In my job, there are metrics. Am I making a positive contribution toward the objectives or am I just riding the wave? As a leader, I am more than a caretaker. I am responsible for achieving the strategic objectives, building stronger teams, and creating a succession plan in preparation for my planned or unplanned departure.

Renewal is what keeps us fresh and makes us wake up with an urgency and hunger to see what life will bring and how we can play a part.

Renewal reduces the Sunday night dreads.

Renewal keeps us curious with a healthy desire to learn and understand. We no longer see things as static truths or laws of nature. We question everything.

Renewal puts a childlike wonder back in our souls. We can once again lie on the ground and look up to the stars and imagine "what if." We can look out across the horizon and dream of lands far away and what might be possible.

Renewal puts old challenges in perspective. Problems that had once seemed insurmountable just may have a solution. What we once considered our list of failures is nothing more than process eliminations. The answer is out there.

Renewal is just what the word says it is—making new again. What do you need to make new again? Start questioning old norms and challenge them with new thinking. Update yourself, but most of all renew the mind. Let's discover the joy in renewal.

CHAPTER 13

The Joy of Moving Forward–
Navigating Difficulties

*"We must be willing to get rid of the life we've planned,
so as to have the life that is waiting for us. The old
skin has to be shed before the new one can come."*
–Joseph Campbell

I f you haven't already reached a point in your life when things just seem to be stale or suddenly stop working, just hang on, you probably will. For most, this is just a natural part of life, due to maturity, lifestyle, or circumstances. In that scenario, we must choose to act. But sometimes the choice to alter our lives isn't made by us.

Sometimes an event occurs, something so traumatic and so severe that reinvention of our plans and selves are mandated without choice. Outside forces swoop in and wreck our plans, our good life, our destiny, so to speak. They leave us feeling cheated, defeated, and outright angry. These circumstances usually have a significant amount of grieving involved. We may blame someone or something for what happened to us–a boss, the economy, a divorce, God, an illness, or maybe the sudden death of a loved one.

This is a book about joy, so you are probably wondering how is this type of change joyous? Bear with me. I never said joy was going to be all fun, but I can promise you it will be rewarding. It's all in how we handle these events.

My wife Stacie tells me, oftentimes sarcastically, that living with me has been an adventure and has required a lot of marriage and life adjustments along the way. We've certainly had our fair share of unplanned "adventure" in our over thirty-seven years of marriage.

When we first got married, we had a typical, simple life planned. You know the one. We would have 1.93 children, a modest brick home, two cars, and maybe an upper middle-income salary. We would be good citizens, help other people. Nothing big. We were just going to work hard, enjoy the fruits of our labor with our grandkids at our feet, and never leave our small town.

Almost none of that happened. Not even close. We left our hometown after ten years of marriage to never move back. We've lived in seven different homes in three states and one foreign country, with at least one more move on the horizon. We did have two kids, but our youngest has Down Syndrome, which changed everything. The quiet job that I planned to work my whole career turned into a corporate job that lasted twenty-nine years and created all those moves. That twenty-nine-year run was disrupted with a new job and another location change at a time when most people are enjoying grandchildren. As a matter of fact, if you place every major adult milestone on a bell curve showing a normal distribution, my wife and I would be the outlier in almost every one of them. We had to pivot, turn, move, renew, and reinvent our plans on multiple occasions. Sometimes we did that well, really well. And sometimes . . . well, let's just say we are still working on it.

My friend Gordie, on the other hand, always navigated life disruptions extremely well. I met Gordie as my limo driver when traveling between the airport and the Mayo Clinic where I was being treated for Amyloidosis. Gordie is a kind, portly man with an infectious smile and laugh. He has thinning white hair and a demeanor that seems to control the room, or in our case, the cab of the limo. From the very first time he picked me up, I was totally drawn into his conversations and loved listening to the stories about his life.

At first glance, it would be easy to believe that Gordie had lived the perfect life. When most of us initially introduce ourselves, we tell only the good parts of our story. He was in his early eighties, fit as a fiddle with a new shoulder—bionic as he called it—and working part-time in his daughter's limo business just to help and stay busy. He has been married over sixty years and said with a chuckle that his secret to a long marriage was to stay out of her way.

Prior to retirement, he had a big farm in Wisconsin. When he ran into a problem with transportation, he started his own trucking company. Then, because there was no way to get anywhere fast from his farm, he built a runway and learned to fly. Not only would he fly himself to needed business adventures but also flew charters for local businesspeople or people wanting to fly to obscure hunting/camping locations. If there was something else he needed to add to the farm or vertically integrate to be successful, he did it.

As a businessperson, I loved hearing of his success and how he worked to grow his business profitably. I thought he had the perfect story and now here he was in his eighties, still enjoying the fruits of his labor. For more than a year, on each ride I would get an additional detail or nugget that I could apply to my own life or business acumen. Finally, one day, after a particularly grueling week and treatment, I wanted to know how he handled setbacks, if he had even had any setbacks. So, I asked him, "What has been the toughest part of your life and career?" His answer brought a richness to his story that I wasn't prepared to hear.

He said the hardest thing he ever dealt with was the death of his son. His intention for building up the farm and the business empire was so his son and three daughters would have an income and a business to run. His son graduated from college with a degree in business in 1979 at the age of twenty-four and married immediately in May. In June, he was fatally electrocuted when he backed up a new grain truck on the farm and swung the grain arm into a power line.

Gordie, his wife, and their three girls continued to run the farm for the next several years. They faced high interest rates in the early '80s, weather set-backs, and the ups and downs of farm prices. But looking back, the farm dream really died for him the day his son died, he said.

The farm was too big to sell as one entity but also too big to run without the help of his son. It took several years for Gordie and his wife to untangle the business and sell it off piece by piece. Once sold, he worked his remaining non-retirement years as a consultant for a seed company.

I could tell as Gordie shared this painful story that he was at peace. I was a wreck. In the strongest voice I could muster, all I could ask was, "How did you do it? How did you go on?" I was immediately putting myself in his shoes. I could not imagine losing one of my sons.

He responded plainly that faith was super important for the day to day coping, but counseling and medication were key to getting both himself and his wife through the darkest days. "Mark," he said, "never be ashamed of needing and asking for help."

Gordie obviously got the help he needed. At some point, he adapted and once again became joyful. He didn't erase or mask his pain, but he didn't wear it like a bumper sticker either. And I had thought his life was perfect, and that he had never experienced a setback when I first met him. Today Gordie builds on that experience by continuing to lead his family and help others navigate similar trials and challenges. He is a blessing to others.

Yes, Gordie has an empty dining room chair as a constant reminder of his grief, but he still smiles and even gets a good belly laugh now and again. He still dreams and plans. Gordie still finds people and the world interesting. He models navigating difficult times and moving forward.

I'm glad I know Gordie. I'm glad I know Gordie's story. Gordie has a life well-lived that I can draw from. He is living proof that a successful life isn't always a perfect life and that bad things can happen. It would have been easy, even natural, for Gordie to give up, quit, lose it all, and finish out his days in misery and defeat. Instead he lived and continues to live a good life. He's still writing his story, but he has secured a good ending.

As I reflected on Gordie's story, my mind drifted back to earlier in my career when I would listen to Earl Nightingale on cassette as I commuted to work. I subscribed to a monthly motivational cassette from Earl's company and would strive to implement the positive messages that he and his team assembled. On one of the recordings, he told a story about a conversation between a farmer and a preacher. The story goes roughly like this. A preacher was driving through the countryside visiting some of his parishioners when he came across a beautiful farm. It was a picture-perfect landscape of trees, crops, and cattle grazing in a knee-deep pasture. There was a neat, beautiful farmhouse and barn with a perfectly manicured garden full of flowers. The preacher stopped in the driveway to look around and drink it all in.

As he gazed over the picturesque countryside, a farmer approached on a tractor. The preacher hollered at him and the farmer stopped, tipped his hat, and asked, "What can I do for you?" The preacher responded, "My good man, God has certainly blessed you with a magnificent farm." The farmer paused, then smiled, looking over his land with pride and joy. He then looked at the preacher and said, "Yes, He has, and we're grateful. But you should have seen this place when he had it all to Himself."

Earl went on to say that the preacher used this experience for his sermon the next Sunday. He likened life to the farm. We are all given a farm, life, opportunity, circumstances. What makes the difference is how we choose to respond and act. The point is not the farm or the number of acres we buy or the land we build on. Instead it is the life we give it, what we do with what we have.

I have recalled the farmer and preacher story several times during my life. Sometimes, I used it in a more cynical way than Earl intended it. I was taking more credit for all the work and discounting the opportunities I had been given. With hindsight and maturity, I now see the problems that I faced were opportunities disguised as hard work. Hard decisions.

Like the farmer and the preacher, I'm sure many looked on Gordie's farm with amazement and said much the same about his farm. "My good man, God sure blessed you with an amazing farm." To which Gordie would readily admit that He sure did. But the life results that Gordie has achieved are not what he had originally planned. There is no textbook formula for life. His success and joy today required a lot of adjustments, self-renewal, and patience.

You and I have and will face similar challenges and obstacles that will require us to stop, pivot, reinvent, and renew. The joy in our story, upon reflection, will be how we dealt with the unplanned, the heartache, and the frustrations. No, we won't find joy in grief. But the end of our story and the process along the way will give us the joy we are pursuing.

You've no doubt had your share of life disruptions already. You are probably listing them in your head right now. We are just told what the norm should be and maybe sometimes we achieve it. But a friend once told me if you put one foot in freezing water and one foot in boiling water, on average you are experiencing the perfect temperature, but it probably doesn't feel very good.

I must be honest here and tell you we did not whistle and smile through every one of our unplanned disruptions. I would even say there were events that we grumbled through and privately wondered "Why?" for a long time. But you know what? As we look back and recall our life as a whole, we wouldn't trade any of these events, as painful as some of them were. They played a large part in making us who we are. These events added the color and contrast to our lives. Like Gordie, they're what made our story rich. It is the pivots, the struggles, the heartaches, the overcoming that has made the journey joyous. Had we stopped, given up, given in, or retreated, our story would have ended. Not ended as with a period, but just ended with an average blah, blah, blah.

For Thanksgiving in 2020, thanks to Covid, my extended family got together via Zoom. I prepared an agenda, being the type A organizer I am. On the agenda, the kids were supposed to tell the coolest thing that happened to them in 2020. The adults were supposed to choose at least two of seven topics that I had given them that pertained to things they were thankful for.

The list to choose from looked something like this:

1. Name a person for whom you are thankful.
2. Name a place for which you are thankful.
3. Name a TV show or movie for which you are thankful that has impacted your life.
4. Name a gadget for which you are thankful.
5. Recall a moment for which you are most thankful.
6. List an experience for which you are thankful.
7. Is there a particular Thanksgiving for which you are most thankful?

The kids were all excited and could hardly wait to tell what they had experienced, despite Covid. We went around the Zoom room and each kid beamed as they told their 2020 event. Their coolest things ranged from biking, hiking, and canoeing, to the oldest one obtaining her driver's license.

When it came time for the adults, I wasn't sure what to expect. I really wasn't even sure what I would share. What turned out to be a theme from every adult was a story of how they had pivoted over an event and became a better, stronger, or more thankful person. Thank goodness we had poor video feed because I think we three brothers were mostly in tears as the stories were told.

My oldest brother summed his up by being thankful for the challenges he faced in the military during the Vietnam war. When he first brought it up, I was thinking, *what? This is what you are thankful for?* I remember witnessing those times. Never knowing where you were going to be stationed. Never knowing if you were going into harm's way. Trying to live as a family in a mobile home in hot west Texas on a military salary. But he described how it had shaped him, given him values, given him lifelong friends, and even blessed them with a family.

Some people, like the preacher in Earl Nightingale's story, see the finished product in a glance and think, *well, you see, they've been blessed with everything.* But Gordie, the farmer, and my own family illustrate that work and reinventing are required to live joyously. When bad things happen, get the necessary help, heal, and do the work you need to do to start moving into a healthier mental state. As a part of the healing, plan and execute what your move forward will look like. There will, and should be, a constant gnawing in your gut as a reminder of the event that marked your life. You're human and that's normal. As we all navigate this life, there will be unavoidable setbacks, challenges, and maybe even tragedies. This much we all have in common. What is not always common but certainly possible is coming out on the other side joyful.

CHAPTER 14

The Joy of Valuing Others–
The 15th Man

"Treat a man as he is and he will remain as he is. Treat a man as he can and should be and he will become as he can and should be." –Stephen R. Covey

My earliest recollection of being ranked or valued was playing on a team in little league baseball. When I was nine years old, my parents asked me if I wanted to go to try-outs. I discussed this with some of my friends and we collectively decided we wanted to play. A couple of my older friends were already in the league playing. Their coolness in a uniform was enough to make me want to join a team.

My mom bought me my first baseball glove to get me ready for tryouts. I was left-handed and up to that point had always worn a right hander's glove but put it on the other hand when we played backyard neighborhood pickup games. We didn't have enough kids for every position but could field enough to have a modified game of sorts with all our shared equipment.

I started breaking in my new glove by putting glove oil all over it and wrapping a baseball in it overnight. I wanted to flex the glove and get the feel for the baseball. Almost every day till tryouts, my buds and I would practice hitting, throwing, and catching. A couple of the older boys who were already in the league would practice with us to help us hone our skills. At this point I didn't know if I was good or not, I just wanted to play the game.

The day came for tryouts when all the coaches would observe from the stands while a couple of other men would hit balls to us to field and throw into the infield or to a base to check our defensive skills. Once a round of that was done, we each had an opportunity to bat through a small bucket of balls. The coaches would draft each of us in a numerical order. We were none the wiser of "how" we did, we were just notified what team we were on and who our coach was.

I was notified of my team and went to my first practice. There were fifteen players, some who had been on the team the previous year, others new to the team like me. We'd usually have two games a week and though only nine would take the field at a time, in the course of the week everyone would get to play at least two innings.

At our second practice we received our uniforms. We each got a cool navy-blue hat and then got in line for jerseys. Jerseys were really nothing more than glorified t-shirts that were mass printed for each team. It appeared that the stack was replenished on a year-to-year basis. They were cheap and in bountiful supply in case one was lost or damaged during the season. They then lined us up for pants in some order that put me dead last in the line. I thought it was alphabetical until I saw a kid with a W last name third in line. I tried to figure out the order as I watched the pants pile get lower. It became apparent that we'd been lined up based on whose kid was whose, such as the coach's kid, and who added the most apparent athletic value to the team. There were only two pairs left when I got my turn—sizes huge and huger. The guy threw a pair at me and told me my mom would need to alter them, but she couldn't make it permanent. They needed to be able to use them as a large pair once I was done with them.

I wanted to cry. Not only did I have a pair of pants that weren't going to fit, I was informally told that I was the fifteenth man on the team. I was last. They didn't expect much of my potential. My mom altered the pants as best she could, and I pretty much lived up to my coach's expectations for the entire year. I generally only got to play the minimal required two innings the league dictated. Even those two innings were predicated by whether we were so far ahead we couldn't lose or so far behind we couldn't win.

In spite of my predetermined ranking, I gave it my all. I pitched, played first base, and played right field. By the end of the season, I had carved out some worth as a relief pitcher. While I did detect some increased enthusiasm in my coaches, it rarely translated to more playing time.

This same scenario played out in my junior high and senior high basketball teams. I again was rated as the fifteenth or least capable (valuable) person on the team. If you look at my seventh and tenth grade basketball team photos, I was the kid with the uniform that didn't match. What was even worse than being fifteenth was the fact that everyone else knew I was thought of as being fifteenth, including the parents and fans.

The pain of these rankings still haunts me, especially when I see kids still being ranked today. Don't get me wrong, I'm not saying give out trophies to everyone and not keep score. What I am saying is give everyone a fair start. Coach them. See what they can do. If we do our part, they will do their part and either soar or we can guide them to something else they aspire to. At least we won't be the reason for their emotional scarring or failure. Who knows what potential great was benched or marginalized before they ever got a chance to shine?

Because of these childhood experiences, I was determined to do things differently as an adult if I ever got the chance. As fate would have it, I got that chance when my own son turned the age for little league baseball. When we arrived to sign him up, I was asked if I would coach. I hem hawed around and told them I would help but probably wasn't qualified to coach. We had just moved to this city and I didn't know the kids or rules, much less the informal rules and etiquette. They said fine and took my name down as an assistant.

A few days later, an acquaintance on the athletic committee called me and said they didn't have enough coaches, and asked if I would reconsider being a head coach. I tried ducking the request by telling him that I would be horrible. I didn't know any of the kids and I would be terrible in the draft trying to pick a team. He assured me it would be no problem, that every team was guaranteed a pitcher and catcher and the rest of the kids were pretty much all the same. So, I agreed, and the committee drafted for me.

To get ready, I called on my buddy Phil to help me coach. He was a young single guy that worked for me and loved kids. He was basically still a kid himself and a great athlete. I figured the kids would identify with him better than me, and we would have the perfect combination of leadership.

Phil and I received a list of our team and phone numbers and called our first practice. After brief introductions, I asked who had played the position of catcher before. No hands went up. I thought maybe they didn't hear me and shouted, "Who has been a catcher before?" Still no hands raised. I figured no problem; we can find a kid that can catch a ball. Let's just find a couple of guys that can pitch.

I announce loudly, "Who's been a pitcher before?" Unbelievably no hands went up, though a couple of kids yelled out, "Coach, I want to pitch!" While I was all for helping these kids reach their potential and would give them a shot, the ones who yelled that out honestly didn't look like they could currently throw a ball that would reach the catcher. We had definitely not been given the experienced pitcher we'd been promised. That's when I realized we had been set up to fail. I found out later the "committee" was primarily made up of other coaches and parents of star kids. I had inherited the land of misfit toys.

Phil, being the eternal optimist and seeing that I was about to faint, suggested we do some pitching and catching warmups and see what shook out. And so, we did, and things started to look a little more promising. A couple of kids could toss a ball and catch. That was a start.

Still, the season went as you'd imagine—we pretty much lost every game. I did do one thing. Every kid had a uniform that matched, and every kid played every game. The kids informally started recognizing who the better players were, but as the coach I made sure there was no distinction of ranking, the way it should be on a team.

It became apparent that I also had the less affluent kids. Kids who were already facing uphill odds in life. Many were from single parent homes or lived with grandparents. My only strong pitcher took me aside one day and said he couldn't make it to the next practice because his dad was in jail and his grandpa couldn't drive. I immediately told him no problem, his house was on my way to practice and I would pick him up. Before the season was over, I practically filled my minivan shuttling the kids from my team.

Phil and I made sure every kid had baseballs to take home and other equipment as needed. After every game, we gave out a game ball to one of the kids. We secretly had a list to make sure everyone got one, but it was in no order. The kids loved it and beamed with pride as they came up in front of everyone to receive the ball. Balls were cheap, self-esteem is not.

Adults and professionals are no different than kids. We don't want to be ranked. And we sure as heck don't want to be ranked last. We want to be given an opportunity and trained to be successful. A fair chance. Much of my career, I have either been a part of the ranked system or was asked to rank my own employees. None of this ever sat well with me.

I would prefer to categorize in terms of those that were excelling and those that haven't yet excelled but were progressing. More times than not, it was usually my fault that an employee failed. I had either not adequately prepared them or I had not guided them to a position or vocation that better suited their skills and passion. My first test professionally on this philosophy was with an employee I'll call Tim. Tim was a leader who was only a few years from retirement. Life and career had taken a toll on him in recent years—his wife suffered from a debilitating illness and he had a bout with cancer until finally being put in remission. He was beaten.

Though I felt sorry for Tim and the things he'd been through, he was absolutely killing us in his job. There were missed plans, missed deadlines. His employees were misdirected, and technology was passing him by. His department had become a wreck and he seemed resolved to live with it. I counseled Tim on several occasions but with few results. When I asked him what I could do to make this work, he became defensive, denying it was really that bad, and saying he just wanted to get by until he retired.

This went on for months with no resolution. For the good of the company to whom I was accountable and Tim's team, it seemed my only option was to let Tim go. However, that would create a moral dilemma for me that I was not willing to face. I could not in good conscience fire an employee that had stumbled in his final years of service. Sure, Tim was partly responsible, but life was too.

Finally, after yet another frustrating day, Tim came into my office and offered to resign. Watching a grown man almost in tears about his job was more than I could take. He said he had wanted to be like Bob, our off-shift manager who had a small team that ran our mini plant at night. Bob was finally retiring and moving on. But that point was still a few years away for Tim—too many years for him to continue as he was. I asked him what his plans were. He replied he had none but figured he could find something. He said he knew he was holding the team back and he didn't want to do that any longer.

When he said he didn't want to hold the team back, my mind went into overdrive. How could I let a team member this self-less walk out my door? I went back to one of my old truths that you can train skills, but you can't train attitude. I thought about what he said about Bob retiring. We were recruiting to find his replacement as our next off-shift leader. Bob's job was as important as any of our front-line supervisors' jobs, but less strategic. Leading the off-shift was strictly tactical. The plans were formulated during the day shift and only execution was required during the night. This is what Tim wanted to do. The strategy and the planning required had passed him by, but he knew he could execute.

"Do you want to take Bob's place?" I almost blurted out to the point of spitting. Tim was shocked at first and seemed unsure. You must remember that all the focus at this point was on what Tim couldn't do. He had lost confidence. I immediately, without realizing, started to affirm Tim. I told him, "You have done all those jobs. You know exactly how they are to be done and you are good at it."

Tim's whole posture started to change. He sat up in his chair and started agreeing. He pointed out how many times he had complained about the off-shift not getting things done right and how he could change that. He also said this shift would work best for his personal life. He could be with his wife and care for her during the day and his son could look in on her in the afternoon while he was at work. We had found a win-win.

Tim went on to do this job and finished out his career a success. He was happy and the team was happy. Through some hard work and positive affirmation, Tim excelled and was one of our best shift leaders ever. He was good at his job. He knew it. We knew it.

There's real joy in valuing others, for the individual, the team, and for you as a leader. Done poorly, or not at all, you will create the fifteenth man. Done genuinely, success will be projected on an individual that they will strive to live up to, inspiring them to excel.

CHAPTER 15

The Joy of Inspiring Others– Inspiration Pollination

"Unleash the potential that is in another and you un- leash the potential that is in you." –Matshona Dhliwayo

Most of us like a little inspiration now and then. If not readily available, we often search for it in a song or an early morning read. We like to have that little boost before we face the day.

But while we like receiving inspiration, if not careful, we can spend little time giving it. If you're like me, intentionally inspiring others doesn't always come naturally. I'm always afraid I will come off as disingenuous or maybe say or convey the wrong thing. My lack of confidence sometimes manifests itself in silence. Not a good thing.

We all know leaders that exuded inspiration, maybe you've even been lucky enough to work for one. These leaders can walk into a room during either celebration or crisis and excite the team to even greater levels. They know just the right mix of encouragement to make it personal for each member of the team. I was fortunate to work with just such a leader early in my career.

It was back in the early 1990s, when there was a huge push for "lean manufacturing." As I mentioned in Chapter 5, during this period U.S. manufacturers were reeling from foreign competition. We had let mass production be our only mantra for success and had become inefficient due to decreased demand. With our own economy shrinking and the pressure of imports, many manufacturers were closing, selling out, or moving to low cost countries.

Lean manufacturing, known by many as the Toyota Production System, was hailed as the best hope of survival for U.S. manufacturing. According to the book *The Machine That Changed The World*, Toyota began perfecting the system after the devastation of World War II. They didn't have the cash and funding to finance the big-batch, large inventory production methods common in other industrialized nations. Being an island nation, they also lacked many of the natural resources with which to build products, and the space to fill factories with lots of inventory. They took all these disadvantages and made their processes leaner by building smaller more cost efficient and responsive factories. Their positive results crippled U.S. manufacturers that were overburdened with cost, overhead, and the need to produce in mass volumes to be efficient.[2]

At this early point in my career, I had already fallen victim to one closed company and was worrying that my new company wouldn't be far behind. I wondered how I was going to

---

2 James P. Womack, Daniel T. Jones, and Daniel Roos, *The Machine That Changed The World* (New York: Scribner, 1990).

support my young family long term. Our corporate office was sending us to seminars, hiring consultants, and printing slogans to make us think lean. It wasn't working. At least not fast enough. Our work group had been successful for many years but was now struggling like many others, searching for what was next. This was when a man named Larry was promoted to take over at the helm. As with most corporate promotions, there was a lot of anxious and not so positive speculation. He was young—what could he know? And he was a bean counter who wouldn't know if his butt was drilled or stamped when it came to manufacturing.

Soon after his promotion, he did his customary visits to all the manufacturing locations for a meet and greet. We had seen this many times. However, this time was different. He wanted to hear from us. He walked the floor, listened to the workers, addressed tough questions, and didn't hide anything. He then asked the plant manager to assemble his staff and did the same Q&A with us. Even though I'm sure we sounded ignorant to a corporate guy, it never showed on his face. He admitted we were in trouble, but we would figure it out together.

The next thing he did stunned everyone, including those in the corporate office. He went to our customers. The same customers that were beating us up on quality and reducing our price every day. They had essentially become our enemy, but he was meeting with them face-to-face asking what they needed, expected, and if they could help us help them. It was not only making waves at the corporate office, but waves in the industry. You rarely ever heard of an automotive manufacturer and a supplier "working together." It had traditionally been a cut-throat and adversarial process. The cheapest supplier, no matter other influences, won the contract. This was such a radical departure from the norm that there were mentions in news articles, and later in books, about his leadership in helping solve an industry-wide problem.

Some of our traditional customers were of little help. They just declared they wanted lower prices and better quality, then sent him on his way. Others offered a little input but seemed too preoccupied with their own issues to work collaboratively. Finally, after completing all the major customer visits, one customer did reach out with an offer to help. Honda of America would allow a team of us to work in their facility alongside their managers and workers on a three-month lean manufacturing project. Once completed, Honda would send one of their senior managers to work alongside us in each of our facilities doing the same process for three more months.

When Larry announced the project and asked for volunteers, we thought he was crazy, or at least a little naive. Our skepticism was that the customer was going to harvest our free labor, come learn and improve our processes, and then ask for the savings in a price decrease.

I reluctantly volunteered as one of the participants to lead a project. As we built air conditioning parts, we were to work in their facility to help install, troubleshoot, and remove waste from their process as it related to our product. At the end of the three months, they would come to our factory and use that same methodology to help us reduce waste, and thus reduce the cost, making us a better, more competitive supplier.

The project was a huge success and groundbreaking as far as supplier/customer relationships. While I did learn a lot about lean manufacturing, what I learned most was leadership and the need to inspire those in your charge. All the volunteers from our organization were young, unsure, and maybe even scared. We had little experience, but we were hungry and desperate to survive. We were a diverse team, male and female, from all walks of life. This, in and of itself, was well ahead of the norms for the time. Larry made sure of it.

I look back on this team of people and wonder what the heck was he thinking? He was leading. He was investing. He was inspiring future leaders and leading us through a challenge that, faced alone, would have resulted in failure. Larry's goal was to not only reduce cost and improve quality, but to create sustainable leadership for the future.

Larry somehow always had the time and wisdom to inspire his team and underlings at every level. He left no one behind as he led from the front. He didn't give out platitudes. His inspiration was pointed, specific, and genuine. You didn't get a participation trophy from him. You earned it. He could address failures head on and give reprimands, but in the end, though feeling defeated, you were inspired to do better.

Larry broke from typical corporate culture. He would often don a sharp suit and tie, but also dressed down to some khakis or occasional jeans and conversed with the doers, the factory workers and plant leaders. He could speak their language and genuinely liked everyone, and we could tell. It was not uncommon for those of us without a title to be cc'd on correspondence addressed to the CEO or the COO about an initiative he was championing. He would routinely include us on corporate correspondence, handwritten notes, or emails, sharing information or congratulations for a job well done. We felt included. We felt essential to the mission.

Turn the clock forward twenty-plus years and you will find many of the then young leaders now leading the charge. They range from corporate executives to entrepreneurs to community leaders. They are the ones who are now creating other leaders. Larry had inspired a generation. He had multiplied his leadership for the future and loved every minute of it.

Larry left this life prematurely in the Swissair Flight 111 plane crash off the coast of Nova Scotia. I can still picture his accomplished smile as he spoke and projected his positive vision for the future. I can still feel the excitement and inspiration thinking of what he was able to create in just a few short years as our leader. Not only did he inspire us, but he inspired others for generations to come.

Just as inspiring leadership can be exponential, so can uninspiring leadership. There are those leaders that surface through organizational inefficiency or inadequacy that not only don't inspire but drain life from their employees. At first it may seem harmless or no big deal, but day after day the inspiration drain will lead to dullness, defeat, and dread. These leaders are usually marked by an ego that requires constant feeding. There is never enough room in their psyche to nurture others. In my experience, most of these leaders could keep a psychiatrist busy for multiple seasons. It has little to do with their people, circumstances, or the organization, and more to do with them as a leader. Fortunately, most of these leaders don't last long. They will typically flame out or create such havoc that their superiors are forced to deal with them and the carnage they inflict.

I once served on a team under one of these difficult leaders. In our case, our leader never socialized or showed a personal interest in us as individuals. All our gatherings as a team usually centered around him and his greatness. Any success that we experienced was attributed to him, while any failures or short-comings rested with us—and he made sure we knew it.

He lived in another city, so we routinely gathered while he was away. While we were starving for vision and direction, we at least maintained a healthy team esteem and accomplished a lot of great things. We were successful despite poor leadership. We would strategize, affirm, and nurture whoever happened to be his latest victim of ridicule. We would often share a chuckle at the ridiculousness of this leader's behavior. While this is not healthy long term, it is a great coping and personal growth strat-egy. In a morbid sort of way, it was fun and rewarding.

If you find yourself in the sphere of negative leadership, don't panic. Give it a little time. While it corrects itself, you can learn a lot from negative leadership. You must also protect your own psyche. You will need to find other sources of inspiration and af-firmation. Many times, you can find this within your own team by nurturing and supporting each other as the formal leader attempts to harvest all the team's energy. You and your team-mates can become the de facto inspiration that keeps everyone motivated, learning, and growing.

Inspiring others is not fixed to a personal profile or title. The recipe for leadership will be different based on your per-sonality. While there are definitely similar characteristics, true inspiration must be genuine and fit the leader dispensing such inspiration. It can come from leaders, young or old, hip or traditional. I'm reminded of another strong leader who was very different from Larry.

When I met this leader, I was in a very different place in my career. I had moved up in corporate management and was now the Global Operations Manager. I was scheduled to be his tour guide for a corporate walk through, visiting all the locations. He was older, and more traditional in his thinking and structure. I remember my initial impression was that he was stodgy, cold, and uninspiring. He gave traditional speeches, dressed only in suit, tie, and cufflinks—always cufflinks—and wreaked of corporate stuffiness. I was dreading our time together and hoped the day would end fast.

As we made our way along the tour at one of our locations, I finished my speech by bragging about the quality and seniority of our employees. This might be the time to mention that I am horrible at remembering dates. I don't remember birthdays, anniversaries, or anything. More than once, I have forgotten my own birthday and needed to be reminded by family. In my defense, I was born on Thanksgiving Day, so I tend to get swept up in all the fanfare of pumpkin pie and family. At any rate, despite my shortcoming I managed to note how many of our employees had been with us ten, fifteen, and twenty-plus years and emphasized that we were known in the community as a good place to work.

As I was about to sit down and turn the mic over to our leader, he asked me to remain standing. He took my arm as he moved to the podium. There he announced to the team that he too had done some research about the team and discovered that today was my twentieth anniversary with the company. He went on to say it was traditional to give out a gold watch for this anniversary date. In front of everyone, he removed his gold watch, put it on my wrist, and told me to wear his until mine was received.

The team was impressed. I was shocked and humbled. Not only had he taken the time to research and learn something personal about me, but he had deflected the meeting from being all about him and focused instead on the mission. He had my attention. He had my team's attention. He was leading. He was inspiring.

Inspiring others really is contagious; it is impossible to contain to only one person. The impact of inspiration is much like the work of the honeybee. The benefit bees provide can't be contained to just one bee or one hive. It's not about the work the bees do collectively to protect their queen and make honey either. That's actually not their greatest importance to mankind at all. It is their work as crop pollinators, spreading pollen from one flower to the next. According to the FDA, those tiny, hard-working bees account for about $15 billion in added crop value.[3] Similarly, inspired humans not only work, live, and prosper within their own circles, but cross-pollinate to everyone around them. It's life giving and sustaining.

We all like to be around inspiring people and will tend to gravitate to them. Successful leaders are purposeful and will go to great lengths to inspire their teams. And their teams are usually crowded, with a wait list for others to join. Money and

---

3 Food and Drug Administration, "Helping Agriculture's Helpful Honey Bees," FDA website, July 30,2018, https://www.fda.gov/animal-veterinary/animal-health-literacy/helping-agricultures-helpful-honey-bees.

job titles become secondary. Growth and personal achievement fuel them and in turn bring energy back to the team and leader. The sum of their parts becomes greater than the whole.

If you aren't inspiring others, start. If nothing else, do it for yourself. It will bring joy to you and your team that will impact generations to come. In case you need help in getting started, here are a few tips:

1. Be enthusiastic.
2. Be careful to be yourself—do not fake enthusiasm.
3. Cast vision and strive to show how each person is an integral part.
4. Show you genuinely care through acts of kindness.
5. Earn their trust by being a person of your word. If you commit —deliver.
6. Build people up. Send notes of appreciation.

Remember, you don't have to become someone else in order to inspire others. Be the person you are best at—you! Let's start an inspiration pollination. The joy of inspiring others never gets old.

CHAPTER 16

The Joy of Tension–
Constant Gentle Pressure

"Tension is the cornerstone of any good story."
–Eric Nylund

Most of us spend a good part of our lives avoiding tension and tense situations. If we are at work and things get tense, we may experience fatigue, frustration, or even anger, and if the situation lasts too long some people will leave their jobs because of it. Our homes and personal relationships are no different. We can handle tension for a season, but if it becomes too uncomfortable or a chronic issue, we often act to address it. This push to action is why tension is not necessarily a negative. In fact, some healthy and balanced tension can bring joy.

One of my colleagues is a lean leader, he focuses on facilitating discussion and action around continuous improvement and the elimination of waste. He refers to healthy tension as Constant Gentle Pressure. This is the kind of tension needed to promote the urgency and necessity of continuous improvement. He sometimes leads a five-day improvement event (a.k.a. kaizen) with a hyper focus on a single issue or problem. The event typically begins with a selection of cross-functional team members who can provide input and action on the identified improvement area. The event follows an order of training, data collection, brainstorming, and implementation. Because of the intense focus and the five-day time limit for implementation and results, the team often feels a sense of pressure, becoming anxious or stressed. This tension is intentional. He reiterates that it's the Constant Gentle Pressure that gets results.

We see how this Constant General Pressure works in many areas of our lives. A few years ago, I decided to establish a routine of working out every morning before work. I signed up with an online trainer who would send daily workouts for me to complete and then provide feedback. It was my job to complete the workout and report the weight, reps, time, etc. so he could track and build on my training plan as I progressed. I had built a small workout gym in my basement complete with weights, exercise bands, treadmill, and exercise bike. As with most of my aspirational pursuits, the planning, dreaming, and scheming were my strongest skills. I thought, *I have all the equipment so how hard could this be?*

I began the program, and at first, I thought I would pass out before I finished my routine. I would report back something like, "barely got through the workout. My muscles were screaming, and I was out of breath at the end of the cardio." I usually received a reply of, "good, that's exactly what we are looking for." Honestly, I thought he was a little over the top. I would remind him that I was over fifty years old and wasn't sure I was cut out for this.

It took the better part of a year of this online training before I "got it." In the beginning of our journey, he had asked me to take some measurements of various parts of my body, including weight. He also had me record cardio times at various distances. I was supposed to update these readings every three months to chart my progress. After the first three months, there was little measurable change other than I stayed sore and tired. I was a little frustrated and skeptical that a fifty-year-old could really improve. It wasn't until completing my ninth month that I noticed real change. I had not lost any weight, as had been my original goal, but had instead become stronger, put on muscle, and had increased my cardio endurance. This was the first time since I started the program that we had done a comprehensive review of my stats. I had mostly been weighing myself and hadn't see much improvement.

I was excited but a little reluctant to report this to my trainer. I had complained most every day about how this wasn't working and now to report success was an "I told you so" moment. I had endured both mental and physical Constant Gentle Pressure, tension, and I was pleased with my results, perhaps even joyful.

Tension can take so many different forms: emotional, physical, even audible. I'm always amazed when watching musicians play. They make it appear to be so natural and effortless. I have friends and family that play music. My wife plays the keyboard, and I believe her to be quite good at it. While I love music, the best thing I play is the radio. I tried to learn guitar, but after lessons and a few years of practice, my best role is still a spectator and listener.

One thing I did learn during this endeavor was the secret to all great songs and musical pieces is tension. The instrumentals or vocals build on the music throughout the song to draw in the listener in anticipation of release. The better the tension of the song, the more exhilarating the release. The writer/musician might do this through rhythm, harmony, melody, dynamics, or other patterns that leave the listener on edge waiting for the crescendo or resolve to make the song ring out in their heart and tug at their emotions.

Take the National Anthem, which we hear at almost every sporting or patriotic event. We experience the tension in the song at the end as it builds in volume and notes that need to be resolved.

> *O say does that star-spangled banner yet wave*
> *O'er the land of the free (note held and pause)*
> *and the home of the brave?*

If timed correctly, the listener sees the fireworks explode and the F-16s flyover to create a swell of emotion and pride. It's hard to be in the audience and not get caught up in the moment as the song concludes. Tension is perfectly released.

At Christmas time, one of my favorite rituals is to have Stacie and my son Jared play and sing "Mary Did You Know?" It usually takes a lot of cajoling, but I eventually win out. Personally, I think they give Mark Lowry a run for his money, but I may be partial. The song goes through several layers of tension as it progresses. The volume is low and subdued as the song describes the birth of the Christ child. As the story progresses there are volume changes, notes that get held, and then a final crescendo of volume and harmony that give into beautiful lyrics for resolution. A believer or not, a listener can't help but be moved by such a piece.

Take note of the music the next time you watch a movie or TV. If it's a scary movie, the music, if well done, helps to create suspense and anxiety to better give emotion to the scene. We are so accustomed and expectant of music with film, that we sometimes take it for granted and it just becomes part of the total experience.

In the old days of having to manually record shows to watch later, I convinced my wife to let me watch Monday Night Football live while we taped *The Sound of Music*. A few days later, when we popped the recording into the VCR, we discovered there was no sound. I had inadvertently used an old compromised tape that recorded the video only. The von Trapp family singers just weren't quite the same without audio. It took the tension that resulted from my error a while to release. We're still married by the way.

The amount and severity of tension is almost always equivalent to the magnitude of the problem. This tension provides the impetus or urgency needed to prioritize and address the problem. Several times in my career I was called on to deal with a crisis. In my early years, these were usually manufacturing plant issues. The plant was either in trouble financially or was sorely behind and customers were being impacted. Those two issues usually went hand in hand—it was rare to have customer issues and not have financial issues or vice versa.

After the first few crisis management assignments, I realized I had become the go-to guy for these situations, which I loved, but after a while I wasn't sure it was worth it. Was there no one else that could do these assignments? I wondered if I was being used, if I was only picked because I was stupid enough to plow through it. Well of course I was being used, but used in a good way. Problems are equal opportunity, and I was in a position to learn how to capitalize on them.

As each crisis presented itself, I would go through the same mental gymnastics. I later was able to identify a pattern in the emotions and stages I experienced:

Pity. *Why was I picked to give up my life and spend the next several months getting this problem solved? Life was going pretty good until this happened. I didn't create this problem. Many things in my life had to go on hold, including the assignment I just left. This seems so unfair.* It's fine to have a pity party just don't camp out there. You have problems—welcome to life.

Anger. *Someone should be held accountable for this debacle, so this doesn't happen again. Who puts people in these positions to fail? Shouldn't this incompetence be dealt with?* Anger is the first response to the tension. Turn this into energy you can use to better assess the problem.

Determination. *If I'm ever going to get out of this, I need to figure something out quickly.* This is that point that I would finally realize the genie lamp doesn't exist and I was responsible. I need to quit moaning and start doing.

Collaboration. *Who can help me that I can depend on to solve this?* This is when I would basically do what had been done to me—yank a couple of my colleagues out of their current assignments to come help. Everything was a team effort. There was no need for a hierarchy or titles.

Solution. *What creative and innovative strategies can we devise to make this problem go away fast?* This is the most fun part of the process. It always amazed me how innovation and solutions can be born out of a crisis. More times than not we revolutionized something that we were able to take with us to use in other applications.

Rapid implementation. *No matter how painful, let's just move mountains and get it done.* Sometimes there is a tendency to wait or take it slow due to the pain inflicted. Dragging out the solutions will only cause more pain and damage. Having experienced several of these challenges, I can confidently advise: just rip the Band-Aid off and deal with it. I would also empower people to act. If a team member saw something that needed doing, they did it.

Celebration. *Wow! We did it? What a relief!* We took this time to reflect on how we achieved success and recognize the key players. Who was cool under pressure? Who was innovative? I subconsciously made mental notes of who I could trust and who could be called on again in times of crisis.

I'm sure a seasoned psychologist can list out these stages in a more clinical fashion, but that's how my layman's mind processed the events.

As I grew as a professional and matured, I learned to see these events and tension more for what they truly were. A growth opportunity. An opportunity to innovate and build new ways of doing business.

I have a good friend who is a private pilot and have had the good fortune to fly with him occasionally for business travel. As we were about to depart one day, he told me that when we arrived we would be landing from a different approach than normal because they were turning the airport around. Not being a pilot, I thought, *what? How do you turn an airport around?* Seems like a lot of work. He went on to explain that due to wind direction changes, sometimes planes have to land from a different direction so there is a healthy resistance to the wings to allow for a safe and successful landing. I always thought a tailwind was good in that it helped you to arrive faster to your destination. I had never given thought to the process of take-offs and landings. Tension and resistance are necessary even for something as big and powerful as a jet aircraft.

I've made a lot of good friends throughout my career. Most of those were formed during times of crisis or tension. I didn't realize that for a long time, but as I put a few years under my belt, I would remember those friends and how those bonds were formed. Sometimes at the end of a meeting or at a party one of my old friends would start, ". . . do you remember when . . ." and then go on to tell some harrowing adventure we had been on only to finish with a laugh and a sigh of reminiscing. Then someone would say, "Those were good times," or "Those were the good ol' days."

Friendship, flying, exercise, music, work . . . there are so many applications of tension, but they all have one thing in common. The effort to lean into and resolve tension is necessary for progress, peace, and success. Resolving tension is a dance. Done gracefully with practice, it yields a beauty and interpersonal growth that allows us to handle bigger challenges with more peace and resolve.

I still do my share of avoiding tension today. That's normal. But remember that tension is where the growth happens, where relationships are restored, and financial stability is achieved. When the opportunity presents itself, seize it. There may be a lot of work to do in the interim, but in the end, there will be joy found in the tension.

Just as my friends and I frequently reflect on the good times, you can too. You will be enjoying the fruits of your labor, but the stories that you smile about won't be the harvest. It will be the struggles, the sweat, the tilling, and planting. It will be the obstacles you faced and overcame. The joy will have been in the season of tension.

CHAPTER 17

The Joy of Humor–
Funny Mishaps

*"A sense of humor is part of the art of leadership, of
getting along with people, of getting things done."*
–Dwight D. Eisenhower

I love humor and have always surrounded myself with people that could make me laugh. Some people have accused me at times of having inappropriate humor, or at least having interjected it at the wrong times, and this may be true. I thankfully no longer use my sophomoric humor, but I must admit, it's not completely gone. I've just refined it a bit. It will still appear when I get together with old high school friends as we reminisce of days gone by. I would venture to guess that a few of our teachers may have secretly enjoyed some of our antics.

The joy in humor is obvious, but did you know there is mounting medical evidence that it has health benefits as well? Humor has been shown to relieve stress, lower blood pressure, ease tension, and improve organ function by increasing oxygen intake. Long-term effects of humor include improving your immune system, relieving pain by creating your own natural painkillers, and lessening depression and anxiety.

I think most people intuitively know this from having experienced the effects of humor at critical times in their own lives. So, if we know it and we've experienced it, why can't we consistently make good use of it? I believe we can, but it's a choice. We must decide to allow humor and to not take this life so seriously.

Joyous humor is never about making fun of another person. Humor at someone else's expense will not only cause you to lose friends and potentially harm someone else, but in the wrong setting will get you sued or fired. However, I have found that self-deprecating humor can go a long way in breaking down barriers and creating authenticity within the team.

I've had a lot of interesting experiences in my life. Some funny and some not so funny, at least at the time. Even the not so funny can make a good story that will make others laugh and break the ice for the start of some good conversation. But first I must be willing to put myself out there for laughter or potential ridicule. For me that's been no problem partly because of our son with Down syndrome. Tate has a way of making you drop social pretense quickly. We do our best to look "normal," but I'm not sure my wife and I know what normal really looks like anymore.

I'll give you an example. Someone once gave me two tickets to a Sunday afternoon Cardinal's baseball game. My intention was to take Tate and make a day of it. When I told him about it, he said, "Nah–just take mom and I will stay home." We figured what the heck, it was a day game and we could be home by dark so what could go wrong? We routinely let Tate have some freedoms but always leave phone numbers or someone to secretly keep an eye on him. Even though at the time of this event, Tate's numerical age was twenty-nine, he is on about an 8th grade maturity level and educational intellect. He's smart enough to get most anything done but not mature enough to always understand the consequences of his actions.

We made plans early on what time we would leave and what time he could expect us to be home. Stacie pointed out to him that there was sandwich meat in the fridge for lunch and grapes for a snack. Tate tends to overeat, so she was stressing his food schedule and the rules.

Tate wasn't thrilled with these options and wanted us to get him a Jimmy John's sub and a cookie. You really haven't seen an argument till you see two redheads go at it, but Stacie prevailed by appealing to his better judgement that making his own meal would be healthier, minus the cookie. That Stacie won this argument was quite a feat since children with Down syndrome tend to overeat, make poor food choices, and use food as a huge satisfier. We should have been more suspicious.

As we drove toward St. Louis, I started to feel bad that we would be eating pretzels and ballpark hot dogs while Tate had lunch meat. Believe it or not, I'm the soft-hearted one in the family. I convinced Stacie before we got too far out of town to repent of her stern ways and go by JJ's to get Tate a sandwich and cookie.

When we returned home with the goodies from JJ's, we opened the garage and discovered Tate's bike was missing. Stacie made a frantic search through the house for Tate while I looked for him on the Find My Friends app on my phone. As we converged back in the garage, we confirmed to each other that although instructed not to, he had indeed left the house. He had also left his phone in his room so he could not be tracked.

Stacie immediately jumped on her bike and headed toward the bike trail hoping to track him down. As she neared the end of the trail where you have to cross a busy street, she saw Tate pedaling his heart out, heading back in the direction of home. Tucked neatly in his back basket was—you guessed it—a Jimmy John's bag with sandwich and cookie. It seemed that now we had two JJ's meals and two cookies.

As they both arrived home, parking their bikes in the garage, Tate had a pained expression on his face. Though I've lost count on the number of times he's been busted for rule violations, he always gives off an air of contriteness and he's very convincing.

The humor in all this was how well Tate had planned this out and how capable he is despite us not always giving him the credit he deserves. Even funnier had to be the workers at JJ's that know us well and our menu choices. They must have been aware that they had just filled the same order for us twice. This is just one of the many "Tate stories" that have kept us real over the years.

The point to this story is it's all in the perception. We could dwell afterwards on our panic and anger. We could bemoan our plight of having a child with a handicap. We could over-react and never let him out of our sight again. We could even wear our misfortune on our faces and be miserable. Instead we choose joy. We choose humor. We know someone is going to get a kick out of this story once our frustration subsides. We know this because we've had a lot of practice. Tate stories are not only funny but almost impossible to hide. So, we just own up to them and let others have a laugh at our expense.

Parenting Tate has always been so much different than our first son, Jared. Besides not having Down syndrome, Jared was born old. He was always sensible, sensitive, and a rule follower. He seemed to understand why rules were in place. Tate, on the other hand, sees rules more as suggestions or guidelines. In all fairness, he knew he was twenty-eight years old and felt (and still feels) that he should be able to do the same things his brother does on his own, including go to Jimmy John's whenever he wanted to. Intellectually, he felt capable of doing the same things and in most cases he is. But for his own safety, because he doesn't intuitively know how to navigate this world, he needs supervision.

We have a friend in Memphis that we met through the Special Olympics that has experienced many of the same mishaps we have. Her son is a few years older than Tate, so we knew what was potentially coming. One day during a swim meet she shared the latest misadventures of her son with laughter. After hearing the story, one of the other parents, who did not have a child with Down syndrome, asked in disbelief why he would pull such a shenanigan. Our friend resolutely responded, "who the heck knows why they do anything!" That's pretty much been our go to line ever since.

I've found humor and problems to be two sides of the same coin. I have experienced timely humor countless times, mid and post crisis. There was always that one thing that seemed to work its way into the story that was able to provide a chuckle. If not embedded in the story itself, it would at least be adjacent to the story.

There are people in my life with the gift of incorporating humor in almost every aspect of their existence. No matter how grave the situation may seem, they can add levity to keep things in perspective. One such individual was a good friend and colleague named Jagg. Jagg worked with me in Quality Assurance for several years as we made our way up the corporate ladder. The number of times we were sent into a tense situation for a good butt chewing are too numerous to count. There were many days after leaving a customer's office that he would have the whole team laughing as we drove to the airport. Even after an especially bad meeting, he was able to at least get us back on an even keel. He wasn't dismissing the problem, but instead getting us over the inflicted pain and anger enough to move towards resolution. This characteristic is a real gift.

Jagg had this same ability to bring levity to his personal life as well. We had a biking team that would meet early on Saturday mornings to train and get in shape to ride the MS-150. The MS-150 was a charity ride for Multiple Sclerosis that would leave Graceland in Memphis and meander through some seventy-five miles of backroads to the casinos in Tunica, Mississippi. We would spend the night in Tunica, then reverse the route back to Graceland the next day.

The ride is held annually in mid-September after Labor Day. Our goal was to have a minimum of eight riders. That made for a good peloton and afforded us plenty of fresh legs to lead the way. We would begin recruiting members for our team in early spring to make sure we had time to raise money and get physically prepared.

Jagg was one of our recruits but never showed up for a training ride. He said he was getting in shape at home and didn't want to make the commute to the training rides. One day I asked him what kind of bike he was riding. He said he was training on one of his kids' bikes but would borrow a real bike for the day of the ride. I told him I wasn't sure that was a good idea and that he would need to make sure the bike fit him well. He blew me off and assured me he would be ready.

The MS ride is broken into seven, eight-mile segments. There is a rest stop with snacks and sports drinks along with support from the local bike shops in the area. The bike shops will make any minor repairs and fix flats to make sure the riders have a trouble-free ride. There is also a sag wagon to pick up fatigued riders or broken-down bikes in each of the segments.

On the day of the ride, we started early in the morning as planned. Jagg had his borrowed bike that looked pretty good. I was starting to think he was more ready than I had imagined as we pedaled away from the start line to begin our journey.

There are several hills on the backroads to Tunica as the route traverses into the delta. Good gearing ratios make all that possible. We were less than halfway to our first rest stop when Jagg's bike locked up in a gear so low that it was almost impossible to ride. This was no problem, the sag wagon simply picked him up and the local bike shop made a quick fix. Well, it wasn't totally fixed, but they restored enough of his gears to at least finish the ride. That mishap would have been fine on its own, but something like this happened at almost every segment. There was an issue with the chain, followed by a flat, then another flat, followed by another chain break and loose handlebars.

We finally all made it to Tunica ready for a good meal and cold beverages. Both Jagg and his bike didn't look any worse for the wear. We jokingly told him that everything on the bike was now fixed and there should therefore be no problems going home.

The next morning, we left Tunica at our appointed time only to have Jagg break down as much or more than the day before. It appeared the rims on his bike were defective and causing flats by pinching the tube inside. The bike shop tried to wrap the inside of the rims enough to get him going. That was only the beginning. He basically repeated almost every problem he had the day before.

At just a few miles from the finish at Graceland, the chain broke yet again. By now, both Jagg and the bike looked beat. He was carrying a few more pounds than a biker should sport, and the bike was being tasked to do a whole lot more than it was capable of. The bike shop had given up on repairing and said a new chain was required - something they didn't have.

When we caught up with Jagg, he was still sitting in the back of the sag wagon with his broken-down bike looking dejected. Trying to find some words of encouragement, all I could say was, "well you almost made it."

"Anyone could do this $h&* if you trained for it," he wittily replied, and then let out a big laugh. Even after all the exhausting and no doubt frustrating mishaps, he was finding humor in his situation, and allowed us to laugh at his misery.

JOYOUS LEADERSHIP • 175

While it may not seem so in the present, difficulties make a great story. Great stories become even better when humor can become part of them. We have all gone through tough times. If we live long enough, we will go through more. It's not my intent to make light of the seriousness of a bad event or situation that occurs in our life. Those things will happen and depending on the seriousness, will take varied amounts of time to process. But let's not forget that humor and problems are two sides of the same coin. When it's time, and that is sooner than you think, flip the coin over. There is humor somewhere in the story.

It is imperative for a leader to know when and how to use humor. Just as humor improves the health of an individual, it has similar effects on teams. Teams must see the humanity of the leader and humor is one of those traits that will help. Properly deployed, humor can add levity to difficult circumstances creating more energy and creativity, thus propelling the team and results to new levels.

Find humor in yourself and this life. Share it with others. Celebrate the joy in humor.

CHAPTER 18

The Joy in Being Lost– Which Way Do We Go?

"Some beautiful paths can't be discovered without getting lost." –Erol Ozan

When I was in senior high, my friend and I used to hunt. In rural Arkansas, it seemed there was always some type of game in season during the school year. Hunting was so much a part of our culture that many of our schools closed on the first day of deer season to allow both the kids and the teachers to be the first in the woods. Times have drastically changed, but back then we had gun racks in our pickup trucks. We would load up our trucks before school with our camo, shotguns, ammunition, and hunting vests so we could leave immediately after the bell rang and get a jump on hunting before dark. I'm not sure I loved to hunt so much as I just loved being outdoors. School season is a beautiful time of the year. I always enjoyed how the evening rolled across the sky with cool crisp air just as we finished our day.

I did most of my hunting with a classmate. He and I shared a lot of interests together. We both owned horses, worked part time at the same grocery store, and were on the varsity basketball team. Shortly after the school year began, we would hunt dove. We had made friends with some local farmers to hunt their fields after the wheat was harvested. We had a place close to school where we could be shooting in less than a half hour after school dismissed.

It was one afternoon after dove season that we decided to hunt for squirrels and rabbits. My family owned a small farm area that housed my horses that bordered some good squirrel and rabbit hunting grounds. This was a little farther from school so we would have to hurry to have much time at all to hunt. We walked to the back of our property and crossed the fence to reach a utility right-of-way. While the area around it was wooded, the right-of-way was kept mowed to allow for utility trucks to drive and service the power lines when needed.

Our plan was to walk up and down the right-of-way in hopes of running up a rabbit or pick off some squirrels retrieving acorns in the trees. We headed up the hill but noticed no movement of wildlife. We then ventured off into the woods to see if we might get a better glimpse of a squirrel. We did this for several minutes, maybe close to an hour, until dusk started to make its appearance. With no luck and not a shot fired, we decided to head back.

We found the right-of-way but couldn't find the fence row leading to our property. We kept walking up and down the right-of-way with no luck. It was getting dark and we were lost. How could this happen? We were both pretty seasoned outdoorsmen and knew our way around this part of the country.

This was long before the day when hunters carried a GPS or could look at their phone and find their parked car. In those days, at most, we carried a compass. If it was daylight, we rarely carried anything. We would mentally note landmarks and keep an eye on the sun and calibrate where we were based on that.

We stopped to take inventory of where we might be. We could still see the glow of the western sky and knew we needed to travel north east to reach the farm. But to do that, would require us to leave our safety zone of the right-of-way. We felt comfortable in this area. We had walked it a dozen times. Were we sure enough to leave?

About the time we had decided to go back into the woods, we heard a car. It sounded like it was just west of us, so we decided to take a sure bet and follow the right-of-way towards the sound of the car. Once we found the road, we would know where we were and could walk back to our truck. It would be longer, but a safer and more certain outcome.

After walking along the right-of-way toward the car sound for what seemed an eternity, we reached a road. It wasn't the road we thought it would be but at least it was a road. We now understood our mistake. We had been walking along a utility right-of-way but not the correct one. We had a faulty path almost from the start. Our lack of attention and over confidence had resulted in a dark uncertain path and a lot of unnecessary walking.

There are times in everyone's life where we feel lost. Sometimes its event driven, and sometimes it's just staleness. Event driven happens when something mostly out of our control totally blocks or significantly alters the path we are on. We may have invested a great deal in our plan and never considered a plan B. We can experience this type of feeling after losing a job, divorce, illness, financial crisis, death of a partner, the list goes on, but you get the idea. It is unpredictable enough that we have no idea how to move forward or find our way back on course.

Being lost can leave us feeling paralyzed, both mentally and physically. Our feet feel heavy while our hearts and minds are cloudy. Our first tendency is to do nothing and hope something appears or happens to prompt us back to home base or normalcy. Sometimes that works but most times it doesn't. We just drift farther into that confused and frozen state.

Being lost due to our life becoming stale or stagnant creeps up on us unnoticed. We are doing the same thing as always, but for some reason it has stopped working for us. Staleness may be mostly our own fault, but the lost feeling it leaves is real nonetheless. We wake up one day suddenly feeling stuck or trapped. We don't know where to turn or what to do next.

The good thing about being lost due to staleness is that you are generally the only one that knows it—at least, in the beginning. To the casual observer, your path still looks well-intentioned and you appear confident in your direction. The fact that no one knows should give us comfort. It tells us it's okay to be lost now and then, and that perhaps we should even expect to be lost occasionally. It allows us to bathe in the feeling and analyze what is really going wrong. Or ask, is anything wrong? It allows time to take a mental inventory and reflect on our feelings and emotions to test them.

Several authors and behavior specialists have attempted to classify a person's stages of life into different seasons or categories. At the core of their models are four categories:

1. Childhood
2. Early Adulthood
3. Middle Adulthood
4. Late Adulthood

Some models further subdivide it to five or seven categories to put a finer detail on the different stages we face as we age. Some of these stages are met with profound staleness, while others may be merely mechanical transitions. Often it is when we are coming to an end of a stage, and are facing the unknown, that a lost feeling can creep in and leave us in a quiet panic.

For me, the childhood to early adulthood was a welcome change. I always wanted to be considered an adult. I've always had dreams and wanted to contribute. My wife says I was born old. I'm sure she meant that as a compliment, at least I've always taken it that way. Starting a career, getting married, buying a house, and having kids were exciting to me. I loved working toward that goal, and I practiced being good at those things. I dove in headlong and gave it my all. I worked hard and invested in my career. I got advanced degrees, joined trade groups, and learned from anyone who would teach me. I didn't consider it work; it was fun. It was a part of my plan. I took the same approach with marriage, kids, and family. All those things were part of a master plan and I was willing to work to achieve it. I coached little league, participated in PTA and school boards, and saved for my children's future. I was following the script.

As I mentioned in Chapter 12, I found that the staleness crept up on me in middle age, and I felt lost, stuck. I didn't know how to navigate out of it. I had to pause, take inventory, check my life compass, pivot, and find renewal to move forward. While most of the life stages have gone as planned for me overall, I won't say they were all simple and worry free. I can think back on many times when I was lost.

The key to preventing or overcoming being lost due to staleness is to recognize and roll with it. Let the next phase draw you in and begin the ride. Once you get a handle of what's going on, re-plan and take control. The major mistake we make is holding on to the past stages, creating stagnation which leads to feeling lost. The stage you just exited is gone but you aren't. You have a new beginning. You can use this for a new start.

But how do we cope with being lost due to an event, when we lose something we treasured—a dream, possession, person, or ideology—that leaves us stunned and in disbelief. What happens when we are forced off the path we know in an unexpected direction?

When our second child was born with Down syndrome, I was lost. As the head of the house, I was supposed to be leading and I had no clue where to begin. I said things in the beginning that were just canned responses that I had learned. A lot of well-meaning people recited some of those same type responses. Sadly, they usually invoked the name of God with their proclamation. "God is good. God is in control. God only gives children like that to special people." All of that may be true in some situations and to some extent, but all it proved to me was they were as clueless and lost as I was. Most of them went home and prayed to God thanking him they weren't in my shoes.

As I stood over my wife after the C-section, I assured her everything was going to be okay. I was lying. I had no idea what to do and wanted to run out of there screaming. I stayed. I made a feeble comment that we would be laughing about this in another month.

Later that evening we sat around with great friends celebrating the birth of our special child all the while privately wondering where the playbook was for a situation like this. We did love the little rascal, but a feeling of paralysis was setting in. We were lost, but at least we were lost together.

Our sadness, disappointment, anger, and denial went on for weeks as we both processed what was happening to our lives. This was something for which we hadn't planned, budgeted, or trained. A few older people with Down's children reached out to comfort us. They meant well, but honestly, as I looked at their lives, I was further lost and a bit more fearful.

A few weeks after Tate's birth we were scheduled for genetic testing. We loaded up the car with our newborn in preparation for our drive to a children's hospital in Memphis. Our plans were to get the testing done and enjoy some Memphis barbeque. While we were planning some fun, at the time it seemed more planning than actual fun.

We were barely out of town when we started laughing about something. I don't remember the topic, but it was probably something dumb I had done. As we laughed, we both looked at each other at almost the same time and in chorus said, "it didn't take a month." We had found laughter and joy in less than thirty days. That wasn't the end to our challenges nor were we never lost again. But we did find there was a way out. We didn't have to remain lost forever. We were on a different path with perhaps different points of interest, but our destination was secure.

The emotions and feelings of being lost were much the same as my friend and I had when we were hunting. It was not a position we planned or wanted to find ourselves in. We were in denial and even a little embarrassed. No hunter or any other human likes to admit they are lost. But we needed to recognize our situation before we could do anything to change our outcome.

As leaders we sometimes get lost. When a company's performance suffers and revenues start to fall, we hear analysts say, "that leader/company has lost their way." Sometimes an indictment like this can mean imminent failure. As with my personal stories above, these lost conditions can be created by outside forces, internal failure, or miscalculation. They can also be the result of stagnation and lack innovation, like the US auto industry faced in the 1990s when they needed to find a new path to keep up in a rapidly changing market.

Once you accept your plight, you can take inventory. Where are you? Look at a compass or landmark. If possible, retrace to where you started. Can you still get to your planned destination? What does that look like? Make a new plan with the best information you have. Move forward. Maybe it will be in a different direction but what's important is that you move. It may not be perfect but take a step and then another. Before long, a day's journey has passed, and you are one day closer to your goal or at the very least, one possibility has been eliminated. It may be slow, but it's progress.

We learn new roads, a new right-of-way, and possibly some new hunting ground. We find confidence in leaving the safe zone and venturing in a new direction. We value more deeply our starting point and awareness of who we are and where we are going. We find joy in the process. We grow from it. We now have a much richer picture to add to our story. Directions can and will only be changed once we're lost and recognize it. There truly is joy in being lost.

CHAPTER 19

The Joy of a Good Name– Better Than Silver or Gold

"A good name is more desirable than great riches; to be esteemed is better than silver or gold." –Proverbs 22:1 (NIV)

W e've all seen people through history pick up a nickname. Generally it's something flattering and attributed to a strong characteristic or trait they possessed. In old movies or TV shows, Slim was slim, Radar had big ears, Shorty was short, and Red had red hair. (This naming of people seemed to have been more of a phenomenon in my parent's time than today.) We see many sports personalities labeled with a name suited for their trade, like Ozzie Smith the Wizard, Walter Peyton Sweetness, Hammerin' Hank Aaron, Pistol Pete Maravich, and of course golfing great Tiger Woods. And then there are the nicknames based on a given name, relationship, or even a toddler's charming attempt to pronounce a difficult name that sticks long after the child has grown up.

When I was in high school, as a matter of respect, we called the male teachers Mister, Brother, or Coach. I attended a small Christian school through all twelve grades, thirteen if you

187

count kindergarten. As with most private schools, the budgets were always tight and much of the staff did double duties. The staff also did without many of the niceties that wealthier school systems enjoyed. We had a fundraiser for everything to supplement basic operating costs.

One teacher we fondly called Brother Moore or Coach Moore. In my junior year, he was a science/biology teacher, coach, and the high school principal. That same year we had a retired preacher and building contractor that served as the senior high boy's bible teacher named Brother Carter. One day Brother Carter slipped up and called Coach Moore, "Tiny," in front of us, a nickname his friends and fellow staff would use affectionately.

Senior high boys all put together in one classroom should never happen. That is just too much testosterone and stupidity for one person to manage, much less a retired preacher and general contractor. Until Brother Carter slipped up, none of us kids were aware Coach Moore had a nickname. Brother Carter would also call the superintendent by his first name. Many times when we misbehaved, Brother Carter would threaten us if we didn't settle down with, "Boys, do you want to go see Harrell (the superintendent) or Tiny?" We'd reply in chorus, "Tiny!"

I should mention that Coach Moore was anything but tiny. He was a giant of a man and was pure solid muscle. Coach Moore would routinely "bump" us boys in the hall and nearly knock us off our feet. He did it with a slight grin and as a reminder of who was in charge. He'd gotten the nickname Tiny while playing football and attending Abilene Christian University. The legend, at that time, was that he was the strongest man they had ever seen. In 1950, Coach Moore's Abilene Christian was the only undefeated collegiate team. He later tried out for the Green Bay Packers but blew out his knee and was unable to continue. Even though his football dream came to an end, the nickname stuck.

As immature teen boys will do, we started using the name Tiny amongst ourselves and around Brother Carter. It was all fun and games till Coach Moore happened to walk down the hall by our open door as we were shouting, "Tiny." He walked into the room, interrupting our so-called Bible class to give us a speech on respect. Coach Moore poured his heart out to convince a bunch of high schoolers that grown men in authority are worthy of respect. They have earned it and that should be acknowledged. He proceeded to instruct us on what names we could use. He said we could call him Coach Moore, Brother Moore, or Mr. Moore but that Tiny was not to be used.

He had our attention. The room was quiet. We were scared and I, for one, was never going to let the name Tiny fall from my lips again. We already respected him, that wasn't the issue. We were just taking advantage of the situation and being knotheaded boys. All seemed taken care of and corrected and Coach Moore seemed satisfied. As he was walking out of the room looking accomplished, Brother Carter called out, "Thank you Tiny!" The room erupted with brief laughter until we got that look from Coach Moore.

The name Tiny, spoken by us kids, was no more. However, I still thought about it over the years. It became less about his size and more an ironic statement concerning his tremendous character. He remained a huge guy and strong as an ox, but it was his humbleness to fill any role in which he was needed that stuck with and impressed me. He was the ultimate utility player. In addition to serving as a P.E. coach, principal, and science teacher, he taught Driver's Ed, Biology, Chemistry, and any other subject that came up short. He was always working around the school doing manual labor, moving chairs and sports equipment, and assisting with remodels. My visual memories of him have more with paint flecks on his face than looking over a dissected pig.

His personal life was just as busy. He served in his local church, attended PTA, and worked his farm. His farm had a huge vegetable garden from which he shared freely, as well as various livestock that included cows, sheep, and pigs. Occasionally some of his jobs intersected and overlapped with school duties. It was not uncommon for the Driver's Ed class to run a few farm errands. One such day, he announced that my Driver's Ed group would be going to a nearby town to get some experience with highway driving. We later found out we were driving him to the livestock auction to pick up a check for some hogs he had sold the previous week.

As you can see, with all the "jobs" Coach Moore had, it would be easy for him to be known by several names. But the name among lifelong friends and colleagues remained Tiny, Tiny Moore.

I stayed in touch with Coach Moore for several years after high school as I attended the local junior college. His wife was my Health and Safety teacher and she truly was tiny and sweet to boot. Talk about opposites attract. I don't know if she had a nickname but, in my mind, whatever it was, they needed to switch.

As a kid, I always wanted a nickname. I had a few friends that had nicknames and I thought it was cool. My grandmother Flora

Louella Watson went by Jim, a nickname my grandpa affectionately used. I used to think it was Gem—in the South, "Jim" and "Gem" are pronounced as the same word. But my brother Larry recently explained, "When she was young, while living in Lepanto, Arkansas, she wore a six shooter on her side and took the nickname from a riverboat gambler." This was a strong woman who did not mess around.

My dad was always called John L. Of course, I called him dad but as a toddler, I remember thinking his middle name must be El or maybe it was a cool nickname. As I grew up and started asking questions about family names, I discovered it was used more as an identifier as there were so many Johns. L was just the initial of his middle name Lawson. I remember this concerning me a little. I was known as Mark, but my name was John Mark. Was I going to be called John M. some day? That didn't sound very cool to a seven-year-old.

Even though not a cool nickname, John L. was known as a good name. I always thought him to be an okay guy, but I didn't grasp the magnitude of this until his terminal cancer diagnosis. In the short time from his diagnosis till death, there was a constant flurry of activity around our house. There were newspaper interviews, TV interviews, tabloid articles, and a civic club honoring him as Law Officer of the Year, just to name a few.

Like most sixteen- to seventeen-year-old kids, I not only thought my dad wasn't cool, but also believed very few people in town even knew who he was. In my view, we were a good blue-collar family but nothing extraordinary. We worked hard, had enough resources to get by, and tried to be good people. We were average as best I could tell. I didn't see my namesake as something I needed to either announce or defend.

For months after his death, I continued to receive attention and hear stories related to his life, most of which I never knew. People that I considered a "big deal" would seek me out and tell me tales about "John L." About the time I thought the legend would fade, something new would spring up and surprise me. At the time, being a teen, I loathed attention from the adult world but still was inwardly proud that my dad had garnered this much respect and admiration from the community.

The accolades not only came from the "big deal" people but from regular people and citizens who had experienced trouble or struggles in life. People who had slipped through the societal cracks. They talked about being treated fairly when served an arrest warrant or sentenced to a few days in jail. They said they had received gas money, grocery money, or a job when no one else would give them a chance.

I sometimes wondered if all these things were true. If so, did my dad know and remember them? It seemed surreal. We never talked about any of this at the dinner table. As a matter of fact, he rarely spoke. How could his life go so fast in front of me and all I had left was his name? I now know I was too young to appreciate a good name. A reputation built over time focused more on actions and less on words. Whether he realized it or not, my father had touched many lives. John L. was a good name. I'm thankful that I have this name in my lineage to be proud of and aspire to.

We all have the opportunity to build a good name. Not only will it bring joy to us now, but it builds a legacy for those that speak of us in the future. And having a good name is essential to being an effective leader. The leader must have established a solid foundation of characteristics on which his team relies. These are not *stated* characteristics but *lived* characteristics. In times of crisis or crucial changes in strategy, sometimes the only collateral a leader has is his name to convince the team to follow and make the necessary changes for a positive outcome. The degree of success oftentimes is a reflection on how good the name the leader has earned.

We've all interacted with, or maybe were, that person that says, "I am who I am and if people don't like me, tough." Or they say hateful or hurtful things and justify it by saying, "I am just being me." That may sound macho and tough, but it's going to be a lonely funeral. This is not to say you are going to go along with everything, including things that compromise your values or morals. But you need to cultivate the wisdom and discernment to know how to act in compassion and discretion, to be of value to others even when doing otherwise would be easier or justified.

It doesn't matter your age, history, or previous character. Having a good name is a daily process. If your name was bad yesterday, it can be good today. The choice is entirely up to you, but the real trick is to start now and add to it each day. There will be mistakes and setbacks, but the trajectory can't be denied.

I have a friend who once suggested that we write our own obituaries. He believed if we were truthful while writing them, we might choose to live differently and make different choices. I like this idea but would challenge you to go one step further. Find some friends or family you trust. They should be of the character that will speak into your life with love and grace, even when painful. Ask them to write your obituary. If they are close and can be trusted, write it together and do it for each other. It can be super affirming and brutally truthful. There will be no doubt things you will be proud of, but there will be pauses, silence, and skip-overs. Focus on where those voids are and maybe there lies your opportunity.

If you find the obituary too morbid, try writing a personal Wikipedia page. Look at some of your favorite notable people with Wiki pages for a guide. Start with a small biography of yourself. Other bullet points can include work history, philanthropic work, beliefs, education, and notable impacts you've made in the community or world. Read through what you write and make note of the edits you would like to see over the next few years of your life. Not only can you make a good name for yourself, but you will essentially have your life plan for the years to come. Would it be a page worth remembering or would it be one in which you would desire a lot of favorable edits. The content going forward is truly yours to write.

Building a name is not like building a commercial brand. You cannot advertise your way into recognition. Tiny and John L. (Brother Moore and Dad) had good names. Neither had a Wikipedia page or desired one, but each built a legacy that was more precious than silver or gold. Their objective wasn't building a name. That was just a byproduct. Their objective was to be a good person and help others in any way they could. A good reputation is earned little by little over time. You can have a good name too. Start now. There is great joy in a good name.

The Last Pitch

I've always wondered how well I could exit a phase of my life. I've always wanted to do it with grace and dignity but wasn't always sure how to make that happen. Thus far, I've always done my best, but what training can you really get for that? Leaving one job to go to another, leaving friends, leaving a hometown, leaving your team, and most of all that final exit of life.

I used to be a pitcher when I played baseball. I pitched left-handed and that seemed to be good for a few innings when most young players during that time had faced few left-handed pitchers. I really wasn't that good, but I loved competing. Because of my love for pitching, I love to watch baseball. The St. Louis Cardinals have always been my team. I've gotten to see some fantastic pitchers over the years in both their organization and others. In the late '60s when I was around ten, I can remember nights when the TV was off, but the radio was tuned to local Paragould AM station 1490 KDRS. Harry Caray called the game and when Bob Gibson was on the mound, Caray spoke of him intimidating the batters as he pitched. There have been several good pitchers since then, but that was my first memory.

When pitchers leave the game there is always a gathering at the mound. Several butt slaps, pats on the back, a lot of glove talking–just an overall send-off for a game well done. Even if the game wasn't so good, it is still a time for congratulating the effort of putting it all out there on the battlefield of play. I always thought that is how I would like to end a career assignment or life event, with a gathering and celebration, but those pitching mound-style send-offs rarely happen. As a matter of fact, they generally don't happen.

How does a person exit a job, assignment, team, or life and do it with humility, thankfulness and grace? I'm still learning. The longest job I've held in my career was twenty-nine years. On my last day, I worked through lunch on some transition papers, unceremoniously left my keys, pass card, and company credit card with my admin, and walked out the door. Hardly a soul knew I left the building. My boss worked in another state and didn't even call to wish me well. As far as I know, the flag went up the next day and there were other people handling my responsibilities as if nothing happened. It was sobering how twenty-nine years could be summed up. Had I really made any contributions at all? Did I make any difference in anyone's life? Was the company a better company for me having been there? Did anyone even notice?

Lucky for me I got to start a new career and use all that reflection for good. Not that I will ever get a pitcher's mound sendoff, but I need to be mentally prepared for that last inning. That last pitch. I wanted to make sure it was a good one. Not just for my company, but for me, for my family. I needed to know that I had done my best. I had given my all. Make plans for that drive out of the parking lot for the last time and know I had pitched my best.

I think this really hit home when I received my diagnosis of Amyloidosis. Before the final diagnosis, it had been narrowed down to three diseases: Multiple Sclerosis, ALS (Lou Gehrig's Disease), or Amyloidosis. When I asked my doctor at Mayo Clinic which of those diseases would be best, he responded soberly, "none of them." He explained at my age, they would all prove deadly and in general, not end well. He sent us home and told me to get my affairs in order. Due to my inability to eat and digest food, my wife and I were sure that I had ALS. My doctor was also leaning that way and had given me a timeline of nine months to a year.

We were stunned. Besides the whole woe is me and feeling sorry for myself, I really began thinking that my life had been a waste. In my mind, I was a mediocre father, husband, son, brother, and business professional. I felt that what few accomplishments I had, really amounted to nothing. I was panicked that this was how fifty-six years of life would end. Nothing.

Once I got over feeling sorry for myself, I turned my emotions toward God. I was mad. How could this happen to our family? Wasn't raising a kid with Down syndrome enough? Sure, I would die and that was going to be a relief, but Stacie would be left with this. I couldn't help but wonder what we did to anger the deity to take this kind of vengeance on us.

About the time all this was going on, the Rory and Joey Feek story was starting to circulate in social media. If you don't know that story, Rory and Joey, country music singers, were raising a Down syndrome daughter when Joey was diagnosed with cervical cancer. My first reaction when hearing their story was anger. Anger that God allowed this to happen to them. Life was not making sense. Haven't some people had enough? Much of my anger I kept to myself but this one made me speak out, at least at home. While Stacie would never try to "set me straight" and even at times I think she agreed, she would usually be the cool headed one and try to diffuse my anger. It wasn't pretty.

One day after coming home from work and going through a hellish day of neuropathy, diarrhea, and constipation, Stacie asked me to read Rory's blog. I thought, *this is going to be just awesome. It's just going to make me angrier.* Then I read it. Here was Rory's entry on October 23, 2015:

So, we don't have forever. We've got right now.

And that's enough.

To say my wife is broken-hearted is an understatement. And to tell you that we're not scared would be a lie. This is the kind of thing that happens to somebody else, not us. But then I have to remember . . . we are somebody else to somebody else.

He goes on to say a paragraph later:

I'm not going to tell you that I'm okay with this because 'God has a bigger plan'. Or that 'we'll understand His bigger purpose somewhere down the line'. That logic doesn't really work for me right now. I'm not angry at God. I'm not angry with anyone. I'm just disappointed. I hoped that Joey would get to be one of the lucky ones that somehow overcome stage 4 cancer and get to hear words like 'remission' or 'cure', instead of 'I'm so sorry'.[4]

---

4 Rory Feek, "Enough," *This Life I Live* [blog], accessed April 22, 2021, https://thislifeilive.squarespace.com/the-blog/enough?rq=enough

There it was. My answer on how to make a good last pitch was contained in my own illness. I had to somehow find a way to change my perspective and life and make it into a great story. And that's what I decided to do from that day forward.

I can't tell you it's all been rainbows and unicorns since that day because it hasn't. I still have days when I've asked God to just go ahead and kill me. Days where I think I can't stand it anymore. No more needles, no more procedures, no more infusions, no more sedation. Enough.

People with terminal or debilitating illness seem to have their own club. It's not a club that we ask to join or even want to join for that matter. It just happens. We find each other and seem to take comfort in one another for the simple reason that we understand each other and have a true empathy for what the other is going through.

The first terminal person to reach out to me post diagnosis was Gary, the husband of one of my high school classmates. I hardly knew Gary on a personal basis, but wow did we connect. He started by sending me encouraging messages and telling his own story via Facebook. His last Facebook post was in 2015 on my birthday, November 27th, posting about the Golden State Warriors. He was a sports fanatic. He lost his fight with cancer forty-three days later on January 9th, 2016.

The club keeps adding members but never seems to grow. As one is added another bows out. How long we stay no one knows. We just know the membership revolves. Even with all the change in membership, we are a tight-knit group. We continue to love, support, and encourage to the last day and welcome new members with loving open arms. The mortality rate is a steady 100%. No one makes it out alive. But those without an earthly diagnosis tend to live as if they are going to be here forever. I know because I used to be one of them.

My pastor friend Josh, a fellow club member who has since lost his battle to colon cancer, used to always asks his friends and parishioners to pray that God be glorified through his illness. It took me awhile to get my head and heart around that request but in my endeavor to have a great story, I too now want to do this.

Wanting a good story and creating a good story are two very different things. It's easy to create a good story when all is good. I see people everyday living a good story. I would even say some are living the dream. But those living the dream are hard to learn from. I needed someone broken. I needed someone working every day at a high-pressure job while simultaneously battling personal health challenges. I needed more Rory and Joey stories.

It was spring of 2015 while channel surfing spring baseball games that I saw a commercial advertising Ernie Johnson Jr.'s *E:60* interview to air on ESPN. I had always admired Ernie on *Inside the NBA* during the playoffs. He, Kenny Smith, and Charles Barkley made NBA game analysis entertaining and fun. For whatever reason, I didn't watch it live, but DVR'd it instead. To this day, I still have it saved.

Ernie is living a great story. Not because of his success as the world measures success. Sure, he has that, but he has so much more. He too was a baseball player growing up, wanting to follow in his father's footsteps in pro baseball. But while in college, time outlasted talent, making journalism with news and sportscasting his future. One would think with his success and fame, his story would be about flashy things. Nice cars, trophy wife, big house, and stuff. Lots of stuff. Instead Ernie and his wife Cheryl are writing a great story.

Besides two children of their own, they have four adopted children, three of whom have special needs. Michael, their first adopted, was born with a progressive form of muscular dystrophy. Even with his disability, that didn't stop them from adopting three more. To add to their challenges, Ernie was diagnosed with non-Hodgkin's Lymphoma in 2006, but continued to work while receiving chemotherapy. Through it all Ernie only missed two golf championships, the British Open and the PGA Championship. Ernie doesn't let circumstances dictate his joy. Charles Barkley said Ernie had "uncommon courage and a pure heart."

During Ernie's cancer treatments he said this about his attitude. "Anytime that fear and anxiety and worry came knocking at my door, I would say, 'You're trying to barge in, but you have to hang out with faith and hope and trust–and they're not going to let you hang around here long.'"

Ernie went on to beat cancer. Through his faith, his love for family, and his continued desire to serve other people, he continues to write a great story. He uses his platform as a renowned sportscaster to help and encourage others to write and live their own good stories.

What is it that allows the Feeks and Johnsons of this world to be different? How does bad stuff happen to them and they make something good come of it? It's faith. Faith that there is more to this life than what we have here on earth. Faith that there is something better. Faith that demonstrates there is something bigger than me. Bigger than death.

So that's where I'm at. I'm trying every day to be like Ernie and the Feeks. Some days I do well and some days I let fear of the future or pain knock me off my intentional path. That's okay. The Great Redeemer makes up the difference, and I move on.

I want to get to the last inning and know that I pitched my heart out. I want others to know that I failed many times but kept on pitching. I want my family to know that as feeble as my attempts appeared to be at times, I tried. I want to know that I made a difference if for no other reason than I tried.

I want my story to have made a positive difference in someone's life. I want my story to help other leaders write a better story. It's never too late to have a good story. Lead joyfully! Live joyfully!

I have fought the good fight, I have finished the race, I have kept the faith. 2 Timothy 4:7 (ESV)

ACKNOWLEDGEMENTS

Thanks to Christina Boys, CEB Editorial Services, for making editing a wonderful experience. Thanks to her coaching, encouragement, and guidance, especially during the times when I would question myself and wonder why I was writing.

JuLee and the folks at W. Brand Publishing, thanks for helping me push this across the finish line. The cover, the layouts, are top notch and make me happy we were introduced.

Ken Haycraft, thanks for offering to produce and mix the audio version of this book. Your excitement for learning and excellence is contagious.

My brothers and their wives have been an inspiration to me from afar. We've rarely lived in the same town but have talked almost daily since being adults. Thanks for being there and supporting my family.

Thanks to the leaders, coworkers, and associates, both past and present, that have shown me grace and helped me learn what true joy is along this journey.

A special thank you to my close friends and fellow alumni of Crowley's Ridge Academy's class of 1977 that would call, text, email, and encourage me. Especially on treatment days when my perseverance would be the lowest. We truly have a wonderful class.

Lastly, but most importantly, thanks to my family who has made this journey joyous. Stacie, my wife, who has worked alongside me to share this journey and pursue our dreams.

Jared, my eldest, that has taught me so much about this life from a whole different generation and perspective. His insights on the manuscript and the creation of my website were invaluable in making this book possible. Tate, our special child, oh to see the world through your eyes. His ideas and input as he would read over my shoulder as I would write could be a whole other book of its own.

M ark is a Paragould, Arkansas native who graduated from Crowley's Ridge Academy, Crowley's Ridge College, Harding University, and has an MBA from Arkansas State University. He is married to Stacie Buck of Paragould and has two sons, Jared and Tate. Mark and family currently reside in Springfield, Illinois where he serves as Executive Vice President and COO for the BUNN Corporation.

Mark loves challenges, both personal and professional. He would prefer to fail at a huge challenge than succeed at an easy challenge. In his career, he has always chosen to do the hard assignments and big challenges. In his opinion, the hard road is where personal and professional growth are realized. Personal challenges began early with the death of his father during his junior year in high school. Next came children and one with special needs. Most recently, a terminal disease diagnosis of hATTR Amyloidosis (also dubbed his superpower) with initial prognosis of less than a year to live. With some luck, love, faith, soul searching, study, and persistence, those challenges have only served to make the journey deeper and more meaningful.

Professional challenges include volunteering for multiple operational and financial rescues, both foreign and domestic, while working for a Fortune 500 company to now leading a medium-sized mid-western manufacturer through growing pains and COVID-19.

He loves competing. He loves building teams. Personal wins include the completion of several marathons, MS150 bike rides, Ragnar Relay teams, and River to River team relays. Professional wins include growing people and building teams to achieve more than they dreamed possible.

Mark believes in giving back and paying it forward. He is always on the lookout for opportunities to do both. He finds making a difference in the lives of others, whether big or small, very gratifying. One such opportunity that is close to his heart is a nonprofit organization for adults with special needs whose mission is to enrich the lives of their clients through housing, work, and relationships.

If you would like Mark to speak to your team or learn more about his journey, please go to www.johnmarkwatson.com and send him a message.

Made in United States
Orlando, FL
01 February 2022

14301762R00122